The

Shadow

of

Christ

*How Jesus Was Foreshadowed
in the Old Testament*

*By
Thomas Cash, M.D.*

The Shadow of Christ

How Jesus Was Foreshadowed
in the Old Testament

By
Thomas Cash, M.D.

ISBN: 0-9747600-0-5

For Beth, Alison and Joseph

"The Lord is God, and he has made his light shine upon us."

— Psalm 118:27

— CONTENTS —

ecause of sin and disobedience, humanity has been separated from God's presence since the fall of man as recorded in the first few pages of the Old Testament. In the fulfillment of time, God sent His Son Jesus to redeem humanity through His death on the cross so that human beings could again enjoy personal fellowship with their Creator.

The New Testament records for us the events in the life of God's Son: His miraculous birth, His wondrous miracles, His divine teachings, and His prophecy concerning the future. Through His birth, God ushered in a new covenant relationship as revealed to us in the New Testament.

But what of the Old Testament Scriptures? Did they merely fill in the historical gap between the fall of man and the birth of Christ? Are they now obsolete and meant to be ignored or discarded? Are they only for the Hebrew people and not applicable to believers living in the twenty-first century? Or was there a purpose divinely woven into the Old Testament that is for our benefit today?

One way to approach studying the Scriptures is to assume that it comprises two volumes: the Old and the New. One might assume that the old covenant was imperfect and needed to be replaced or corrected by an improved covenant—the New Testament. Therefore, God sent His Son to supplant it and begin an improved new covenant. The problem with that line of reasoning is that God's Word is not imperfect! "The word of the Lord is flawless" (Psalm 18:30). Therefore, the Old Testament is not something that is in need of replacement or correction. So what is the purpose of the Old Testament for us today?

One of the most powerful and effective methods that Jesus utilized to impart truths during His life on earth, as recorded in the New Testament, was the use of stories. For example, on one occasion an expert in the Law (Old Testament) asked Jesus, "Who is my neighbor?" (Luke 10:29). Instead of directly answering the man's question, Jesus told the illuminating story of the Good Samaritan and then asked the expert the same question, "[Who] do you think was a neighbor?"

The Bible in its entirety is the story of God's Son, Jesus. The arrival and teachings of Jesus and His death and resurrection from the grave were events that God did not want humankind to miss. Therefore, God prepared us for the advent of His Son through the stories comprising the Old Testament Scriptures.

"All the world's a stage, And all the men and women merely players." Those words of Jaques in Shakespeare's *As You like It* embody what God was doing through the Old Testament. God orchestrated the events in the lives of many of the Old Testament personalities in the way that Shakespeare would conduct a play. God's divine purpose was to reveal to us prophetic information through many of the Old Testament stories so that we would not miss the coming of His Son.

The theological term for prophecy that is revealed through an event or story is "typology." The event is called a "type" and its prophetic fulfillment is referred to as the "shadow." The New Testament's recording of the life of Christ was, therefore, the shadow of many Old Testament types.

In the classic spy movie, a spy was prepared to meet a secret agent by receiving special information: the location and specific time of the agent's arrival, a description of the agent, the agent's mission, and possibly some code words. Throughout the Old Testament

Scriptures, God has prepared us for the arrival of His "agent" as well. We are told the specific time and place of His arrival. We are given some information about His appearance. We are informed about His mission. And there are some code words for us as well.

These code words involve the prophetic types God uses to reveal information about His Son. This book will attempt to explain some of the numerous Old Testament types of Jesus Christ. Our mission is to search and examine the Old Testament types of Christ so that we may better understand Him and His mission.

— CHAPTER ONE —

HEALING FROM A SHADOW

As a result, people brought the sick into the streets and laid them on beds and mats so that at least Peter's shadow might fall on some of them as he passed by. — Acts 5:15

"I want to ask my doctor a question before you put me to sleep!" The woman's request caught me by complete surprise. It came at the last possible moment before the anesthetic was to be administered, rendering her unconscious in less then sixty seconds. She was lying on a cold, hard operating room table about to undergo a sophisticated and delicate eye surgery on a detached retina that threatened her vision. The unanticipated request brought our normal routine to an abrupt standstill. As we awaited the arrival of her surgeon, our forced inactivity (combined with an awkward silence that loomed in the air) caused our few moments of delay to feel like an eternity.

In the silence, I began to wonder what she was so determined to ask her surgeon before drifting off into the realm of anesthesia. Maybe she wanted him to review the possible complications of the procedure. Or possibly, she wanted a last-minute reassurance that her vision would be restored. The fear of the unknown is sometimes the greatest of fears; and she had more than her share. Would she be able to see again? Would she feel pain during the operation? Would she awaken from the anesthesia? I could only imagine the thoughts that were going through her mind and the question she so desperately needed answered.

My mental wondering ceased suddenly as her surgeon walked into the operating room and took his place by her side. Now the unanticipated question that had intruded upon our routine and aroused such curiosity was about to break the room's silence. All eyes were on the patient; and all ears were eagerly tuned in anticipation.

"Are you a Christian?" she inquired of her surgeon. For the second time, this lady had caught me by surprise. Her question was not at all what I had anticipated. Awaiting his reply, all eyes and ears simultaneously refocused on the surgeon.

His answer was immediate and without hesitation. "Yes Ma'am, I am," he professed. Then he added something that still warms my heart to this day, "I only put things back where they belong. *God does the healing.*"

Modern medicine, with all of its pride and prestige, had been summed up with four words of reassurance and comfort: "God does the healing!" Physicians can treat diseases, such as hypertension, diabetes, and emphysema; but we can't cure them. We can transplant a heart; but we can't cure heart failure. We can remove a cancerous segment of the intestinal tract; but we can't cure cancer or cause the wound edges to grow together. As sophisticated as medicine is today, we can't even cure the common cold! God does the healing. The same God who created us heals us in accordance with His plans.

The Healings of Jesus

As Jesus went about during His earthly ministry, He was constantly performing miracles; many of them involving healings. We obtain some insight into the sheer magnitude of His miracles from the apostle John when he wrote: "Jesus did many other things as well. If every one of them were written down, I suppose that even the whole world would not have room for the books that would be written" (John 21:25). The Scriptures inform us that Jesus healed people of blindness, paralysis, leprosy, and even physical death!

Given the extent of His miracles, one might wonder why certain healing miracles were recorded in the Holy Script, as opposed to His innumerable miracles that were omitted. The apostle John further illuminates this for us in John 20:30-31: "Jesus did many other miraculous signs in the presence of his disciples, which are not recorded in this book. But these are written that *you may believe* that Jesus is the Christ, the Son of God, and that by believing you may have life in his name" (emphasis added). In other words, there was a reason for selecting the specific healing miracles that were recorded. They were chosen that we might *believe* in Jesus and have salvation. The primary concern of Jesus was salvation, healing from spiritual death. Ultimately, spiritual healing was the divine purpose for including the specific healing miracles in God's Word.

Spiritual Healing

We gain more insight into spiritual healing from reading the second chapter of the Gospel of Mark. Here, Jesus is preaching in a house located in the town of Capernaum. We are told that some men brought their friend on a mat to be healed of his paralysis. Because the crowd was so great and they could not get into the house through the door, they climbed onto the roof, made an opening, and lowered him down to Jesus. *Their* goal was to have Jesus heal their friend; but notice *Jesus' concern* for the man: "When Jesus saw their faith, he said to the paralytic, 'Son your sins are forgiven'" (Mark 2:5). The forgiveness of sin, *spiritual healing*, was *Jesus'* primary concern for this paralyzed man, not the healing of his paralysis!

As seen in the following quotation, Jesus proceeded to heal the man of his paralysis, fully knowing the thoughts and beliefs of those about to witness the event, in order to prove to those present that He had the ability to forgive sins:

> Now some teachers of the law were sitting there, thinking to themselves, "Why does this fellow talk like that? He's blaspheming! Who can forgive sins but God alone?" Immediately Jesus knew in his spirit that this was what they were thinking in their hearts, and he said to them, "Why are you thinking these things? Which is easier: to say to the paralytic, 'your sins are forgiven,' or to say, 'Get up, take your mat and walk'? But that you may know that the Son of Man has authority on earth to *forgive sins...*" He

said to the paralytic, "I tell you, get up, take your mat
and go home." (Mark 2:6-11, emphasis added)

In Jesus' day, the Jews believed that illness was the result of some
sin in one's life. This is evident from the following passage: "Rabbi,
who sinned, this man or his parents, that he was born blind?" (John
9:2). It is a good question because if physical illness resulted from
personal sin, how could someone be born with a disease? Therefore,
it would be reasonable to assume that the man's parents had sinned.
Jesus knew that people believed physical illness resulted from sin.

Therefore, in the minds of those present, the paralyzed man's condition must have resulted from his own sin. And since his physical
illness was due to his own sin, if he could be forgiven then he could
be cured—or so thought the Jews. In order to prove that He indeed
had the power to forgive sin, Jesus healed the paralytic, so in minds
of onlookers that meant his sins also had been forgiven. Notice Jesus'
primary concern: It was the *spiritual* well being of the man. Jesus
healed the paralytic, "that you may know that the Son of Man has
authority on earth to forgive sins."

Another example of Jesus' concern for spiritual healing is demonstrated when Jesus heals ten men of leprosy (Luke 17:11-19). This
passage reminds me of an archeological dig. As you sift along the
surface, you easily can see the healing miracle involved; but if you
dig deeper, there is a hidden treasure to be found involving a second
miracle. The second miracle happens to be the greater of the two
miracles. Let's dig in and see if we can find the greater of the two.

Jesus was on His way to Jerusalem when He encountered ten leprous men standing at a distance outside a village. Old Testament
Law (Leviticus 13:45-46) required them to maintain a distance from
the village. The men cried out to Jesus to have pity on them; He told
them to "Go, show yourselves to the priests." This also was in accordance with the Law. If someone was healed of their skin disease, they
had to go and be examined by the priest to be pronounced clean
(Leviticus 14:1-4).

This then, became a test of faith for the ten leprous men. They
first had to believe that Jesus could heal them of their leprosy; and

then obediently go and present themselves to the priests to be declared clean. As the ten went on their way they were indeed healed of their leprosy, and then an interesting thing happened:

> One of them, when he saw he was healed, came back, praising God in a loud voice. He threw himself at Jesus' feet and thanked him—and he was a Samaritan. Jesus asked, "Were not all ten cleansed? Where are the other nine? Was no one found to return and give praise to God except this foreigner?" Then he said to him, "Rise and go; *your faith* has made you well (Luke 17:15-19, emphasis added).

Again we see Jesus' concern and emphasis on the *spiritual condition of the man—his faith.*

The buried treasure here is found in the meaning of that last word— *well.* The Greek word used here is *sozo.* The word *sozo* is used 106 times in the New Testament; but only twice is it translated as "well." The most common translation (occurring eighty-two times) is the word saved. What Jesus said to this thankful man lying prostrate at His feet was the same thing He said to the sinful woman, who was also at His feet, in Luke's gospel, "Your faith has *saved (sozo)* you" (Luke 7:50).

We encounter the word sozo in the following passages as well:
- "Whoever believes and is baptized will be *saved.*" (Mark 16:16)
- "Whoever enters through me will be *saved.*" (John 10:9)
- "Believe in the Lord Jesus, and you will be *saved.*" (Acts 16:31)
- "For it is by grace you have been *saved,* through faith." (Ephesians 2:8)

Therefore, Jesus' statement to the healed Samaritan leper alternatively might be translated, "Your faith has saved you." This hidden miracle, the Samaritan's salvation, was the greater of the two.

Notice that the nine Jewish lepers, who also were healed of their leprosy, did not return to thank Jesus or give praise to God. They were so typical of the Israelites of their day. They could accept Jesus' miracles; but they could not accept Him as their Messiah.

The primary concern of Jesus then, was spiritual healing; the beginning of which is salvation. The provision of salvation was the reason for Jesus' incarnation. "For God did not send his Son into the world to condemn the world, but to *save the world* through him" (John 3:17, emphasis added). The apostle John informs us that the healing miracles were recorded "that you may believe that Jesus is the Christ, the Son of God, and that by believing you may have life" (John 20:31). The "life" that John was referring to is the spiritual life that we have by believing and placing our faith in Jesus as the Son of God. At the moment that we receive Jesus as our personal Savior, the Great Physician heals us of a terminal illness—spiritual death. By His saving power we are raised from spiritual death and given a spiritual rebirth.

Spiritual Healing Continues

Jesus no longer physically dwells among us, but He continues to accomplish spiritual healing through His followers. Physicians are but mere instruments that God works through to accomplish physical healing. Christians are spiritual physicians God wants to work through to bring about spiritual healing to all humanity! Jesus performs the miracle of spiritual healing by working through Christians who are equipped with the Sword of the Spirit—the Word of God. "He sent forth his word and healed them; he rescued them from the grave" (Psalm 107:20).

Types and Shadows

After Jesus was no longer living among His followers in fleshly form, we are told in Acts 5:15-16:

> As a result, people brought the sick into the streets and laid them on beds and mats so that at least Peter's shadow might fall on some of them as he passed by. Crowds gathered also from the towns around Jerusalem, bringing their sick and those tormented by evil spirits, and all of them were healed.

The Scriptures are curiously silent as to whether healing actually occurred as a result of Peter's shadow. We are therefore compelled to contemplate whether someone can actually receive healing by a shadow.

As we have already established, the greatest form of healing is spiritual healing; so we are led to ask—is there a way to receive *spiritual healing* from a shadow? I believe there is. It involves a theological concept called typology.

Typology is the study of one form of prophecy. There are basically two forms of prophecy that occur throughout the Old Testament. First, there is the spoken word of God, where God *speaks* through His prophets. For example: "The word of the Lord came to me, saying..." (Jeremiah 1:4). The second form of Old Testament prophecy is contained in the *events* of the lives of the Old Testament persons themselves. This is what is known as types and shadows. Typology, therefore, is the study of types and shadows.

The Old Testament event is called the "type," and its prophetic meaning is the "shadow." This involves an understanding that God was orchestrating events in the lives of the Old Testament personalities, as recorded in the Holy Scripture, to guide us toward understanding what He would do in the future. In other words, God used the types in the Old Testament to cast their shadows throughout history in order to give us a better understanding of Christ and His purpose, both in the New Testament and in the times yet to come!

Jesus Used Typology

Jesus used an example of typology during His earthly ministry. In Mark 8:11-12, we are told, "The Pharisees came and began to question Jesus. To test him, they asked him for a sign from heaven. He *sighed deeply* and said, 'Why does this generation ask for a miraculous sign? I tell you the truth, no sign will be given to it'" (emphasis added). Imagine Jesus, the creator and sustainer of life, God incarnate *sighing deeply*. What was it, do you suppose, that caused our Lord Jesus to sigh deeply? The answer is found in the rest of His answer to the Pharisees that Mark's account fails to include.

Up to this point in the Gospel of Mark, Jesus had cast out evil spirits, healed leprosy and paralysis, raised Jairus' daughter from the dead, and miraculously fed the multitudes; and yet the Pharisees still did not believe. In effect, what the Pharisees were saying to Jesus was, "We have seen your miracles and we are not impressed that you are who you claim to be—the Son of God. Show us something that will impress us to believe."

I purpose that Jesus *sighed deeply* because, as we read His complete answer to the Pharisees in the Gospel of Matthew, there was still a miraculous sign yet to be performed; and it was the thought of that sign that caused Him to sigh deeply. Let's take a look at Matthew's account of what Jesus said. "A wicked and adulterous generation asks for a miraculous sign! But none will be given it *except* the sign of the prophet Jonah. For as Jonah was three days and three nights in the belly of a huge fish, so the Son of Man will be three days and three nights in the heart of the earth" (Matthew 12:39-40, emphasis added).

Jesus sighed deeply because He was yet to perform the ultimate sign—His death and resurrection on the third day. This sign would become a crisis of belief. It would prove beyond any doubt that He was indeed God's Son. The Pharisees may not have believed that Jesus was the Son of God based on the miraculous signs that He had performed up to that point, but the sign of the prophet Jonah, Jesus' death and resurrection, would be the final and ultimate sign. If they believed in that sign, they would be saved. Perhaps this is the meaning in Paul's statement, "If you confess with your mouth, 'Jesus is Lord,' *and believe in your heart that God raised him from the dead,* you will be saved" (Romans 10:9, emphasis added).

So Jesus Himself gave us an example of types and shadows. The events in the life of the prophet Jonah were actually prophecy concerning events in the life of Jesus. Jonah was trapped in the belly of a great fish for three days and miraculously came forth alive and shared the message of God with a Gentile nation. Upon hearing God's message, the Ninevites repented and were saved from the coming destruction. Likewise, Jesus was in the tomb for three days and miraculously came forth alive. The message of God was then shared with the Gentiles (Book of Acts). Therefore, if we repent, we also will be saved from the coming destruction.

Typology Links the Old and New Testaments

Saint Augustine understood the importance of typology, saying, "The New Testament is in the Old contained; the Old Testament is in the New explained."[1] In other words, events in the New Testament were present in the Old Testament through foreshadowing; and the Old Testament is explained by the events of the New Testament.

Paul tells us, for instance, concerning the various wilderness experiences of the children of Israel: "These things happened to them as examples and were written down as warnings for us, on whom the fulfillment of the ages has come" (1 Corinthians 10:11).[2] The Greek word that is here translated as "examples" is the word *typos* from which we get the English word "types." Therefore, Paul is stating that the events of the Exodus were types that were orchestrated by God for our instruction.

Likewise, we are told in Hebrews 10:1: "The law is only a *shadow* of the good things that are coming" (emphasis added). Jesus explains, "If you believed Moses, you would believe me, for *he wrote about me*" (John 5:46, emphasis added). Furthermore, Jesus said, "Do not think that I have come to abolish the Law or the Prophets; I have not come to abolish them but to fulfill them" (Matthew 5:17). Here Jesus is saying that He is the *fulfillment of the entire Old Testament.* Jesus' reference to the "Law" refers to the first five books of the Old Testament, the Torah, which are known as the "Books of the Law." The remaining books of the Old Testament consist primarily of the writings of the Prophets.

We are told in 1 Corinthians 15:3-4, "Christ died for our sins *according to the Scriptures,* that he was buried, that he was raised on the third day *according to the Scriptures*" (emphasis added). What Scriptures was Paul talking about? It could not have been the Gospels because they had not yet been recorded when Paul penned his first letter to the Corinthians. The "Scriptures" Paul was referring to were the Old Testament verses.

You may ask, "Where in the Old Testament does it discuss Jesus?" The answer—*throughout the Old Testament!* God was orchestrating the events in biblical history for the purpose of revealing information about Christ. As we shall see, instead of *history* we probably should refer to the Old Testament as *His Story*!

Jesus Explains His Story

In Luke 24, we read that after His resurrection, Jesus appeared to two of His followers as they were traveling to the village of Emmaus. After revealing Himself to them, He explained to them all that had been written about Him in the Old Testament: "And beginning with Moses and all the Prophets, he explained to them what was said in all the Scriptures concerning himself" (Luke 24:27). Not a word of the New Testament had been written as Jesus spoke to His followers at Emmaus. The "Scriptures concerning Himself" were from the Old Testament.

Therefore, we understand that the Old Testament contains types, which serve as *portraits* of Christ, which allow us to better understand Him and His purpose. There is silver plate that exists in a museum somewhere that illustrates this concept well. The plate has the words of the Constitution of the United States engraved upon it in such a way that it resembles the face of George Washington. Up close, you see the words that make up the doctrine of a nation; far away, you see a picture of one of our founding fathers. The Old Testament is much the same as that silver plate. Up close you see the words that make up the laws and doctrines of the nation of Israel; but if you back up and look carefully, you can behold images of Christ.

Our task is to be like the Berean Christians. In Acts 17, we learn that the Bereans were described as having "more noble character" than the Thessalonians because they "examined the Scriptures every day to see if what Paul said was true." The "Scriptures" they examined were the Old Testament Scriptures—that was all that they had. In other words, as Paul was sharing the gospel about Christ with the Bereans, they were searching the Old Testament Scriptures to validate Paul's testimony!

We also need to examine the Old Testament and understand what it imparts to us about Christ. If we are to fully comprehend the entirety of what God's Word has to say about Christ, we need to harvest messianic information from both the Old and New Testaments. Otherwise, we may emulate Jesus' disciples as they beheld the empty tomb: "They still did not understand from *Scripture* that Jesus had to rise from the dead" (John 20:9, emphasis added). Once again they were deficient in understanding the Old Testament Scriptures.

Perhaps Clarence Larkin said it best when he stated: "Therefore no preacher or Bible Teacher is competent to preach the doctrines of the New Testament who is not acquainted with the "Typology" of the Old Testament."[3]

The Shadow of Christ

So how is it that we can receive spiritual *healing* from the types of Christ that are contained in the Old Testament? As we are able to see Christ more clearly, we develop a better understanding of Him and our salvation. A shadow is but a reflection. We can't look directly at Jesus today; but we have His reflection from the shadow of His Word. The Scriptures reveal to us the presence of Christ in the New Testament and His foreshadowing in the Old Testament. The better we understand Christ, the *living Word of God*, the healthier we will be spiritually! In other words, our spiritual health depends upon our understanding of Christ; and the beginning of spiritual healing is salvation.

Saved By a Shadow

Can someone be saved by a shadow? Let me share a true story with you.

> The crack British express train raced through the night, its powerful headlamp spearing the darkness ahead. This was a special run because it was carrying Queen Victoria and her attendants.
>
> Suddenly... the engineer saw a startling sight! Revealed in the powerful beam of the engine's headlights was a weird figure loosely wrapped in a black coat that was flapping in the breeze, standing on the middle of the train tracks, waving its arms, a signal

to stop! The engineer immediately grabbed for the brakes and brought the train to a screeching, grinding, sparks-flying halt!

Then the engineer, his assistant, the coal tender, and a couple of conductors climbed down to see what had stopped them. They looked, but they could find no trace of the strange figure. But on a hunch, the engineer walked a few yards further down the tracks. Instantly he stopped and stared into the fog in horror! The rainstorm, which passed through the area earlier in the evening, had caused the bridge to wash out in the middle span and it had toppled into the storm-swollen stream! If he had not paid attention to the ghostly, weird figure, the train would have plunged into the overflowing stream … with how many lives lost or bodies mangled, who knows? The engineer was so overcome with the emotion of the near miss that he sat down on the tracks for a few moments before making his way back to the idling steam engine.

Word was wired for help. And while the bridge and tracks were being repaired, the crew again made a more intensive search for the strange flagman, unsuccessfully. But it wasn't until they got to London that the mystery was solved.

At the base of the steam engine's headlamp, the engineer discovered a huge dead moth. He looked at it a few moments … then, on impulse, wet its wings and pasted it to the glass of the headlamp.

Climbing back into the cab … he switched on the lamp and saw the "flagman" in the beam. He knew the answer now; the moth had flown into the beam mere seconds before the train was due to reach the washed-out bridge. In the fog it had appeared to be a phantom figure, a flagman waving his arms signaling the train to stop!

Later when Queen Victoria was told of the strange happenings she said, "I'm sure it was no accident. It was God's way of protecting us."[4]

The passengers on that train were literally saved by the shadow of a moth. They were completely oblivious to what was happening; and had the engineer not noticed the shadow that was cast, they would have met with certain destruction! Likewise, there may be some of you reading this book who have yet to know Jesus Christ as your personal Savior. As your engineer on this journey, I want to cause you to stop and see some of the shadows that have been cast down through the Old Testament types. As Queen Victoria said, they are "no accident." They are God's way of protecting us by allowing us to see the One who can save us from eternal destruction.

Others of you reading this book may be secure in your salvation. You may be like those Greeks who came to Philip and said, "Sir, we would like to see Jesus" (John 12:21). All of us should desire to see Jesus more clearly, and God has painted a portrait of Jesus Christ throughout the Scriptures to enable us to do so.

The portrait, however, is a puzzle that we must put together. The New Testament pieces of the puzzle are easily placed. The Old Testament pieces are harder to find. But with the help of God's Holy Spirit as our Guide, we may be able to put together many of the puzzle pieces so we can see more clearly the big picture that God has prepared for us. We won't be able to fill in every piece, as Jesus did for His two followers on the road to Emmaus; but hopefully we can fill in enough to get a better glimpse of the picture painted for us by the very hand of God. As God was orchestrating the events of the Old Testament, He was painting for us a beautiful *masterpiece*. It is up to us to search out the "Master's pieces" so we can behold His beauty!

Eyes to See

We are not unlike that patient who wanted her vision corrected so she could see more clearly. Our problem though, is not a detached retina—we need spiritual vision! Just as Elisha's servant could not *see* the chariots of fire poised and ready to do battle until God opened

- 23 -

his eyes (2 Kings 6:17), we also need God to open our spiritual eyes. Just as the patient was comforted by the words of her physician that, "God does the healing," we can be comforted that the Great Physician will help us to see the Master's artistry more clearly!

We find ourselves like those early believers on the road to Emmaus. We are on a journey to a greater understanding of Christ by learning what was foreshadowed about Him in the Old Testament. As you study this material, my hope is that you may, like those two followers on the Emmaus road, exclaim, "Were not our hearts burning within us while he talked with us on the road and opened the Scriptures to us?" (Luke 24:32b). May you also receive their blessing: "Then he opened their minds so they could understand the Scriptures" (Luke 24:45). My prayer for our journey is that we, like the ill who waited for Peter on the side of the street, may receive healing from the shadows that come our way!

— CHAPTER ONE QUESTIONS —

1. Regarding the miracles of Jesus, the author states: "There was a reason for the selection of the specific healing miracles that were recorded." What might have been God's reason for selecting the following miracles?
   a. Healing blindness (Consider John 9:1-5,39)
   b. Healing paralysis (Consider Mark 2:1-12)
   c. Healing leprosy (Consider Luke 17:11-19)

2. While John the Baptist was in prison, he sent a message to Jesus inquiring, "Are you the one who was to come, or should we expect someone else?" In view of your answer to question one, why do you think Jesus answered John's question as He did? (See Luke 7:18-22)

3. How could Jesus' answer to John the Baptist relate to the passage from Isaiah that He read while in Nazareth? (See Luke 4:16-21)

4. Jesus explained that the "sign of the prophet Jonah" (Matthew 12:38-40) was a foreshadowing of His death and resurrection. What event in His life did the "snake in the desert" (John 3:14-15) foreshadow? (See Numbers 21:4-9)

5. What is the significance of the "men of Nineveh" and the "Queen of the South" mentioned by Jesus in Matthew 12:41-42? How do they apply to contemporary Christians?

6. The death and resurrection of Jesus were referred to as His "ultimate sign." How could the passage in 1 Kings 17:17-24 concerning the widow of Zarephath's son foreshadow this concept? Compare the widow's response to that of the disciple in John 20:8.

THE LAMB OF GOD

Behold, the Lamb of God, who takes away the sin of the world!
—John 1:29, RSV

Hardening of the arteries," a condition known as coronary artery disease, leads to heart attack and heart failure. In fact, it's one of the leading causes of death in our day. "Hardening of the heart" is, likewise, *the* leading cause of spiritual death!

Throughout the Old Testament, the Israelites suffered from a hardened heart, the result of rejecting God's Word. "They made their *hearts as hard as flint* and would not listen to the law or to the words that the Lord Almighty had sent by his Spirit through the earlier prophets" (Zechariah 7:12, emphasis added).

The apostle Paul explains the outcome of a hardened heart:

> So I tell you this, and insist on it in the Lord, that you must no longer live as the Gentiles do, in the futility of their thinking. They are darkened in their understanding and separated from the life of God because of the ignorance that is in them *due to the hardening of their hearts.* Having lost all sensitivity, they have given themselves over to sensuality so as to indulge in every kind of impurity, with a continual lust for more. (Ephesians 4:17-19, emphasis added)

Paul describes spiritual death as being "separated from the life of God." Clearly, the rejection of God's Word, the *hardening of the heart,* is the leading cause of spiritual death.

A Hardened Heart — A Case in Point

God's desire is that no one should have a hardened heart. So would He ever *intentionally* harden someone's heart? A close look at the Book of Exodus reveals that God has done so. You probably know the story; but let me set the stage.

God appeared to Moses in the land of Midian where he had been in exile from Egypt for some forty years. God tells Moses that he is to go to Pharaoh of Egypt and demand the release of God's people, the Israelites:

> You are to say everything I command you, and your brother Aaron is to tell Pharaoh to let the Israelites go out of his country. But *I will harden Pharaoh's heart,* and though I multiply my miraculous signs and wonders in Egypt, he will not listen to you. (Exodus 7:2-4, emphasis added)

Here we have a paradox that is easily passed over. If God wanted to free His people from bondage in Egypt, why would He intentionally harden Pharaoh's heart so he wouldn't let the people go? This is one of those difficult questions of the Bible.

An equally difficult question for many is, Why would a loving God ask Abraham to sacrifice his son Isaac? These questions may appear difficult on the surface, but when you understand what God is doing through types and shadows, the answers take on prophetic meaning. Through the prophecy of types and shadows, as recorded in the Old Testament, God—the Master Artist—used the events in Israel's history as His canvas and Scripture as His divine paintbrush, painting for us a beautiful portrait of the Lamb of God!

By hardening Pharaoh's heart, God was demonstrating for us that He was in complete control and personally orchestrating the events of the Exodus. God hardened Pharaoh's heart in order to reveal prophetic truths through the plagues He brought upon Egypt. If Pharaoh had allowed the Israelites to leave before the plague of the firstborn occurred, there would have been no Passover plague. God used the Passover plague to give us a glimpse of Christ and what He ultimately would do!

The Passover Lamb

The Israelites were commanded to take a year-old lamb, either from the sheep or the goats, and keep it tied up on display for four days. The lamb was to be without spot or blemish. At twilight after the fourth day, they were to sacrifice the lamb, paint its blood on the doorframes of their dwellings, then roast the lamb over the fire and eat it. That same night the firstborn of everyone whose house was not "sealed" by the blood of the lamb suffered death. However, the firstborn of those who obediently placed the lamb's blood on their doorframes were saved.

This was salvation by the blood of the lamb! It required faith and obedience in following God's command. They had to *obey* (by placing the blood of the spotless lamb on their dwellings) and then have *faith* that God would do as He promised (sparing the lives of their firstborn).

The Passover is a picture of our eternal salvation by the blood of the Lamb of God. Our salvation also requires faith and obedience. We are saved from spiritual death by our *obedience* to God's command to place our *faith* in the blood of Christ, the Lamb of God, which was shed for us on the cross. It is what we sing about:

Just as I am without one plea
but that thy blood was shed for me
and that thou bidst me come to thee
Oh Lamb of God I come, I come.[1]

A Sacrifice Required

In Genesis 15—18, we find the account of God's promise to Abraham and Sarah. God promised to give the elderly couple a son whose descendants would be as numerous as the stars in the sky and the sand on the seashore—but the child didn't come for a very, very long time. On three different occasions, God repeated His promise to them concerning the birth of a male heir. Year after year passed and the child did not come. Sarah was an elderly, post-menopausal woman of ninety before God fulfilled His promise and allowed her to give birth to a son—Isaac.

Why did God make them wait so long? And why, after waiting so long for their only begotten son, would God ask Abraham to sacrifice Isaac as a sin offering? The answer to these tough questions, as I explained earlier, is that God used these events to show us a fore-shadowing of Christ.

Isaac was a child of promise just as Christ was a child of promise. "For to us a child is born" (Isaiah 9:6). Christ was born of a virgin birth through divine intervention of God. Isaac's birth also involved the divine intervention of God. Ninety-year-old women don't give birth! Therefore, God obviously intervened. There are those who doubt the truth of the virgin birth. Perhaps God allowed Sarah to wait until she was ninety years old so there would be no doubt that the birth of Isaac, a foreshadowing of the birth of Christ, was accomplished through the divine intervention of God.

Foreshadowing the birth of Christ is also the reason why God commanded Abraham to sacrifice Isaac, his only son. God also would sacrifice His only begotten Son—Jesus. This is a type of what Jesus would do on the cross to fulfill His role as the Passover Lamb. Arthur Pink in his book, *Gleanings in Genesis*, explains, "This is the only type in the Old Testament which distinctly intimated that God required a *human* sacrifice. Here it was that God first revealed the necessity for a human victim to expiate sin, for as it was man that had sinned, it must be by man, and not by sacrifice of beasts, that Divine justice would be satisfied."[2]

"Then God said, 'Take your son, your only son, Isaac, whom you love, and go to the region of Moriah. Sacrifice him there as a burnt offering on one of the mountains I will tell you about'" (Genesis 22:2). Pink points out that, "Here, as nowhere else, are we shown a wonderful foreshadowment of the *Divine* side of Calvary. Oh! How the Spirit of God lingers on the offering and the offerer, as if there must be a through similitude in the type and the antitype— '*thy son—thine only son—whom thou lovest*'! Here it is we learn, in type how that God 'spared not His own Son' (Romans 8:32)."[3] The Master Artist uses such detail in this type that it is hard to miss its shadow. Indeed, the shadow of the cross with the Lamb of God hanging on it is the very foundation of our faith!

The region of Moriah was a mountain range that contained a hill of historical significance. Upon this hill was the threshing floor of Ornan, which God requested David to purchase (2 Samuel 24:24). David's son, Solomon, built the first temple on this same site (2 Chronicles 3:1). After that temple was destroyed, a Muslim shrine was built there. That shrine is called the Dome of the Rock. The rock over which the Dome is built is reputed to be the very place upon which Isaac was bound for the sacrifice. This hill is also the site of the place we call Calvary. Thus Christ was sacrificed on the same hillside where Isaac was bound for the sacrifice! What extreme detail God used in this type of the crucifixion!

"Abraham took the wood for the burnt offering and placed it on his son Isaac, and he himself carried the fire and the knife" (Genesis 22:6). Pink points out that, "This was no half-grown boy (as pictures so often represent Isaac), but a full-grown man who is here brought before us, one who could, had he so wished, have easily resisted the aged patriarch."[4]

Here again the Master Artist, with a stroke of His divine paintbrush, has given us more details about the shadow of the Lamb of God. Isaac carried the wood to his place of sacrifice in the region of Moriah, just as Christ carried the wooden cross to His place of sacrifice at Calvary on Mount Moriah. Just as there was no protest from Isaac (he willingly allowed the aged patriarch to bind him for the offering), Christ uttered no protest but willingly allowed Himself to be bound to the cross. "He was led like a lamb to the slaughter, and as a sheep before her shearers is silent, so he did not open his mouth" (Isaiah 53:7, emphasis added). Jesus said, "I lay down my life—only to take it up again. No one takes it from me, but I lay it down of my own accord" (John 10:17-18).

"Isaac spoke up and said to his father Abraham, 'Father?' 'Yes my son?' Abraham replied. 'The fire and the wood are here,' Isaac said, 'but where is the lamb for the burnt offering?' (Genesis 22:7). Abraham's answer to this question contains only a few words, but what a masterpiece God paints through them! There are multitudes of beautiful paintings hanging in the museums of the world, but none compares to the beautiful picture God paints through

Abraham's reply. As I ponder Abraham's great faith in God and his great love for his only son, I imagine Isaac's question caused their journey to stop momentarily. I picture Abraham as he fought back the tears, peered deep into the eyes of his only son, and said past the lump in his throat, "God himself will provide the lamb for the burnt offering, my son" (Genesis 22:8). *God will provide the Lamb!* What a masterpiece we behold in the truth that God would provide the Lamb for the sin offering!

When they reached the place that God had told them about, Abraham built an altar there and arranged the wood on it. He bound his son Isaac and laid him on the altar. Then he reached out and took the knife to slay his son. But the angel of the Lord interceded and stopped Abraham from sacrificing his son.

There are many angels mentioned throughout the Old Testament but this one, called "the angel of the Lord" (Gen. 22:11), was a special messenger. It was the Angel of the Lord who spoke to Moses from the burning bush and led the Israelites through the wilderness by a pillar of cloud. *Nelson's Bible Dictionary* explains, "The Angel of the Lord performed actions associated with God, such as revelation, deliverance, and destruction; but he can be spoken of as distinct from God. This special relationship has led many to conclude that the Angel of the Lord was Jesus in a pre-incarnate form."[5]

To fully comprehend this, we must understand that Jesus Christ did not come into existence some 2000 years ago when He was born as the Christ child. He has always existed. We are told in John 1:1-2, "In the beginning was the Word, and the Word was with God, and the Word was God. He was with God in the beginning." In other words, John explains to us that Jesus is not only the *Living Word of God,* but He is also a part of God and is omnipresent!

Assuming the Angel of the Lord was indeed a pre-incarnate manifestation of Christ, then it was Jesus who stopped Abraham from sacrificing Isaac! Imagine Jesus, the Lamb of God, having His portrait painted by God, the Master Artist who paints with the words of Scripture. Jesus was there to give His personal touch to this masterpiece!

The Lamb of God

Jehovah-Jireh — "The Lord Will Provide"

As these events unfolded on the hillside of Moriah, God made Himself known to Abraham as Jehovah-jireh, meaning, "The Lord Will Provide." Abraham did not intend to trick Isaac when he said, "God himself will provide the lamb." Abraham, our father in the faith, truly believed that God would somehow provide the lamb.

As Abraham saw Moriah from a distance, he left the two servants behind with these last words: "We will worship and then *we will come back to you*" (Genesis 22:5, emphasis added). Abraham had complete faith in God's provision and Jehovah-jireh did indeed provide the lamb! After Abraham was stopped by the Angel of the Lord, "Abraham looked up and there in a thicket he saw a ram caught by its horns. He went over and took the ram and sacrificed it as a burnt offering instead of his son" (Genesis 22:13).

The Painter's brush has given us a few more details in this masterpiece. For the Passover sacrifice, the Israelites were allowed to take either from the sheep or the goats. Here we see a male goat, or a ram, with its horns in the thicket, or thorns. This perfectly foreshadows Jesus, the Lamb of God, with a "crown of thorns" on his head!

The Big Picture

Let's step back from the brush strokes and behold the portrait as a whole. The promised child—an only begotten son born through divine intervention—carried the wood for the sacrifice to the hillside of Mount Moriah and willingly allowed himself to be the sacrifice. The true sacrifice had its head crowned with thorns. Jehovah-jireh has indeed created a masterpiece!

This passage of Scripture ends with some words addressed to Abraham from the Angel of the Lord: "Through your offspring all nations on earth will be blessed, because you have obeyed me" (Genesis 22:18). If Jesus was indeed the Angel of the Lord, He is concluding this work of art by telling us about its shadow—*Himself!*

Jesus is the promised "offspring" born in the lineage of Abraham and Isaac! He is the Shadow of Life that would bless those living in the shadow of death mentioned by the prophet Isaiah: "The people walking in darkness have seen a great light; on those living in the land of the shadow of death a light has dawned…For to us a child is born, to us a son is given, and the government will be on his shoulders. And he will be called Wonderful Counselor, Mighty God, Everlasting Father, Prince of Peace" (Isaiah 9:2, 6). When you are surrounded by darkness, you can't see any shadows. Jehovah-jireh provided more than the portrait of the Lamb of God as a foreshadowing. He also provided the Light of the World, Jesus Christ, who allows us to behold the foreshadowing and through whom all nations have been blessed.

Foundation of the Sacrificial Lamb

To fully understand the necessity for the sacrificial lamb, we must go back to Genesis 4. It is here that the Master Artist laid the foundation for the "Lamb of God, who takes away the sin of the world" (John 1:29, RSV).

It's no coincidence that this passage follows the "fall of man" as described in Genesis 3, which ends with man being driven out of the Garden of Eden and cherubim blocking the way back to the tree of life with a flaming sword. Because of sin, man was now separated from the presence of God.

We are then told: "In the course of time Cain brought some of the fruits of the soil as an offering to the Lord. But Abel brought fat portions from some of the firstborn of his flock. The Lord looked with favor on Abel and his offering, but on Cain and his offering he did not look with favor" (Genesis 4:3-5). Notice first that this was an act of worship. They brought their offerings *before the Lord*. We are, therefore, given insight as to what sacrificial offerings please the Lord. The focus here is not on the *men themselves*, but on the *offerings* they brought before the Lord.

We should not be surprised that Cain's offering was unacceptable to the Lord. First of all, it was from the ground or "the fruits of the soil." We had just been told in Genesis 3:17, "Cursed is the *ground* because of you" (emphasis added). Secondly, it was a bloodless offering.

Hebrews 9:22 informs us, "without the shedding of blood there is no forgiveness." Lastly, it was the work of his hands, the fruit of his labor. Ephesians 2:9 instructs us that salvation is "not by works, so that no one may boast."

Abel's offering, on the other hand, was acceptable to the Lord. Notice that Abel's offering was brought from the "firstborn of his flock." Here we see the need for the sacrifice of an innocent lamb. In this passage, we have the foundational strokes of the divine brush that would later add the Passover plague of Egypt and the substitution of the ram for Isaac to the overall picture of salvation.

Salvation by Grace — Not by Works

In Genesis 4, we have a foreshadowing concerning the doctrine of salvation. "For it is by grace you have been saved, through faith—and this not from yourselves, it is the gift of God—not by works, so that no one can boast" (Ephesians 2:8-9). We cannot save ourselves. There is *nothing* we can do to earn our salvation. Like Cain, the fruits of our labor will not be acceptable to the Lord. As Isaiah expressed, "All our righteous acts are like filthy rags" (Isaiah 64:6).

We must have faith, like Abel, in the Lamb that Jehovah-jireh has graciously provided. The writer of Hebrews explains, "By faith Abel offered God a better sacrifice than Cain did. By faith he was commended as a righteous man, when God spoke well of his offerings" (Hebrews 11:4). Notice that it was the *offering* that made Abel a righteous man. When we receive Christ as our Savior, the blood of the Lamb of God covers our sins. As a result, when God looks at us He sees the acceptable offering of the Lamb, not our sins! "God made him who had no sin to be sin for us, so that in him we might become the righteousness of God" (2 Corinthians 5:21).

The focus now shifts away from the offering to the one providing the offering. Cain was angry that his offering was not acceptable to the Lord. "Then the Lord said to Cain, 'Why are you angry? Why is your face downcast? If you do what is right, will you not be accepted?'" (Genesis 4:6-7). His offering was not acceptable, but he is told that if he does what is right, he will be accepted. In other words, if we do what is right—if we commit no sin—then there is no need for a sin offering and we will be acceptable to the Lord. The problem is that no one can do what is right. Romans 3:23 explains to us that, "*all* have sinned and fall short of the glory of God" (emphasis added). Cain would have been acceptable to God if he could have done what was right. However, Genesis 4:8 vividly portrays that Cain could not fulfill the requirements: "Cain attacked his brother Abel and killed him" (Genesis 4:8).

Jesus Christ was the only one who could meet the requirements; He committed no sin, yet He traded places with us so that we may be acceptable to God. The firstborn of the flock, the Passover lamb, and the ram with his head caught in the thorns all foreshadowed Jesus—"the Lamb that was slain from the creation of the world" (Revelation 13:8).

Jesus Fulfilled the Prophecy

Look at how beautifully and accurately Jesus fulfilled the foreshadowing prophecies of the sacrificial Lamb of God. He was crucified during one of the annual feasts. It was no coincidence that it was the *Passover Feast*. Jesus was the Passover Lamb!

Jesus rode a donkey into Jerusalem on the day we call Palm Sunday. This was the fulfillment of Zechariah 9:9: "Rejoice greatly, O Daughter of Zion! Shout, Daughter of Jerusalem! See, your king comes to you, righteous and having salvation, gentle and *riding on a donkey*" (emphasis added). That first Palm Sunday was also in fulfillment of Daniel 9:25: "Know and understand this: From the issuing of the decree to restore and rebuild Jerusalem until the Anointed One, the ruler, comes, there will be seven 'sevens' and sixty-two 'sevens.'" Grant Jeffrey writes, "This period of time, beginning with the command to rebuild the walls of Jerusalem (March 14, 445 B.C.) until the Messiah was 'cut off' (April 6, A.D. 32, the tenth of Nisan) is seven 'sevens' plus sixty-two 'sevens', equaling sixty-nine 'weeks of years' (173,880 days). This prophecy was fulfilled to the exact day."[6]

To add more significance to that first Palm Sunday, the Passover Lamb was to be selected on the tenth of Nisan and was to be kept for four days until it was sacrificed on the fourteenth of Nisan (Exodus 12:3-6). The purpose of keeping it on display for four days was so that it could be examined and proven to be without blemish. Therefore, it was no coincidence that the day Jesus made his "triumphal entry" (the tenth of Nisan) was lamb selection day!

Although we herald this event as the "triumphal entry," Jesus' temperament seemed to be anything but triumphant. "As he approached Jerusalem and saw the city, he wept over it" (Luke 19:41). Why did Jesus weep? He didn't weep because they missed His coming as their Messiah; they didn't miss His coming at all. Matthew 21:9 tells us, "The crowds that went ahead of him and those that followed shouted, 'Hosanna to the Son of David!' 'Blessed is he who comes in the name of the Lord!'" The Hebrew word "Hosanna" means "salvation" or "save us." One of the titles for the Messiah was "Son of David." What they were saying was, "Save us, Messiah!" Then they quoted Psalm 118:26, "Blessed is he who comes in the name of the Lord." They didn't miss the coming of the Messiah; but they did *miss His purpose!* He was fulfilling the role of *the sacrificial Lamb of God.*

Sadly, their rejection of Him would fulfill Scripture as well. It is interesting that as the crowds were shouting from Psalm 118:26, they were skipping over a prophetic verse just four verses before! "The stone the builders rejected has become the capstone" (Psalm 118:22). Jesus wept over Jerusalem because He knew these same people who were shouting "Hosanna" on the tenth of Nisan would be crying "Crucify Him!" just four days later—on the day of Passover!

Furthermore, just as the Passover lamb was placed on display for four days, Jesus taught in the Temple, in full public display, for the four days between His "triumphal entry" and His crucifixion. No fault of any kind was found in Him. Jesus was indeed the "spotless Lamb without blemish," selected by God to bear the sins of the entire world once and for all!

Lastly, just as Isaac willingly submitted himself as the sacrificial offering, Jesus willingly became the fulfillment of the Passover

Lamb. He was in complete control of the events leading up to His death on the cross!

For example, Jesus told His disciples that He would be crucified on Passover: "As you know, the Passover is two days away—and the Son of Man will be handed over to be crucified" (Matthew 26:2). But the chief priests didn't want to arrest Him during the Passover: "Then the chief priests and the elders of the people assembled in the palace of the high priest, whose name was Caiaphas, and they plotted to arrest Jesus in some sly way and kill him. *'But not during the Feast,'* they said, 'or there may be a riot among the people'" (Matthew 26:3-5, emphasis added). The fact that Jesus was crucified on the very day of Passover, as He predicted, even though it was not the desire of those who arrested Him, proves that He indeed was in complete control of the events that were transpiring. Jesus said, "I lay down my life—only to take it up again. No one takes it from me, but I lay it down of my own accord" (John 10:17-18).

The Passover Meal — A New Meaning

On the night of Jesus' arrest, He celebrated the Passover meal with His disciples. This is the meal that Christians commemorate as the Last Supper. The Passover meal was a Jewish meal of remembrance concerning the events of their release from bondage in Egypt. The meal consisted of the roasted paschal lamb, unleavened bread, and wine. We have already expounded on the fulfillment of Jesus as the Passover Lamb.

Jesus proceeded to explain to His disciples that He was the fulfillment of the Passover meal.

> And he said to them, "I have eagerly desired to eat this Passover with you before I suffer. For I tell you, I will not eat it again until it finds *fulfillment* in the kingdom of God." And he took bread, gave thanks and broke it, and gave it to them, saying, "This is my body given for you; do this in remembrance of me." In the same way, after the supper he took the cup, saying, "This cup is the new covenant in my blood,

which is poured out for you." (Luke 22:15-16, 19-20, emphasis added)

Jesus changed the meaning of this Passover meal's remembrance. From that time on, they should not remember their deliverance from bondage in Egypt; instead they should remember what that first Passover was foreshadowing: Jesus Christ, the Lamb of God who freed us from bondage to sin and death. From that time on, Jesus requested that the Passover meal be observed *"in remembrance of me"* (Luke 22:19). The apostle Paul reiterates: "Whenever you eat this bread and drink this cup, you proclaim the Lord's death until he comes" (1 Corinthians 11:26).

The Scapegoat

The pieces of the divine artist's picture are coming together so that we can, as John the Baptist proclaimed, "Behold the Lamb of God." But there is still one piece of the puzzle yet to be placed.

Thus far, we have examined the shadow of the Lamb of God that was slain. Yet there is another lamb that deserves our attention as well. We meet this lamb in the fall feast of Yom Kippur, also known as the Day of Atonement.

The Day of Atonement was the one day each year when the high priest was allowed to enter the Holy of Holies to make atonement for the sins of the nation of Israel. The sin offering for the nation of Israel consisted of two goats. First, the high priest would offer a bull as a sacrifice for his own sins. Then he would take two goats and cast lots on them. The goat upon which the lot fell would be sacrificed as a sin offering for the people. Its blood would be sprinkled on the mercy seat of God. The other goat was called the azazel—the "scapegoat."

In their book, *The Fall Feasts of Israel,* Mitch and Zhava Glaser give us insight into the meaning of the scapegoat. "The root of the word azazel contains the idea of removal. The name azazel and the action of sending away the goat was designed to teach the Israelites that their sins, once removed, would also be forgotten." In Jesus' fulfillment of the scapegoat we have an understanding of the forgiveness of our sins. "As far as the east is from the west, so far has he removed our transgressions from us" (Psalm 103:12).

The Glasers also point out:

> A parallel to the azazel is the ceremony of cleansing a cured leper. Two birds were chosen, one to be killed and the other to be dipped in its blood. The live bird was then released, symbolizing to all that the curse of leprosy was totally removed from its former victim (Leviticus 14:1-9). The birds were considered one offering, teaching the lessons of cleansing by blood and removal of the affliction.
>
> Similarly, the two goats were viewed as one offering: "And he shall take from the congregation of the sons of Israel two male goats for *a sin offering*" (Leviticus 16:5, emphasis added). The slaughtered goat showed the congregation that God's wrath was appeased, while the live goat was sent into the wilderness bearing the sins of Israel, illustrating that they had been removed (Psalm 103:12).
>
> This "scapegoat" was just as much a sin offering as the goat that was slaughtered....The two goats foreshadowed the sacrifice of Christ. When the Messiah died on Calvary, He paid the penalty for our sins, as did the goat that was slaughtered. He also removed sin.
>
> ...John the Baptist combined the idea of the azazel with the Passover Lamb. Standing on the stones of the Jordan River, John cried: "Behold, the Lamb of God who takes away the sin of the world" (John 1:29). Jesus is not only the slain Lamb who protects us from the wrath of God (Exodus 12), He is not merely a "sheep led silently to the slaughter" (Isaiah 53), He is also the azazel (Leviticus 16). For through His death, the sins of all who believe are completely removed."

Philip Explains that Christ Is the Lamb

In the eighth chapter of the Book of Acts, Philip, one of Jesus' disciples, encountered an Ethiopian eunuch. "The eunuch was reading this passage of Scripture: 'He was led like a sheep to the slaughter, and as a lamb before the shearer is silent, so he did not open his mouth. In his humiliation he was deprived of justice. Who can speak of his descendants? For his life was taken from the earth'" (vv. 32-33).

When Philip asked the man, "Do you understand what you are reading?" the eunuch replied, "How can I unless someone explains it to me?" We are told, "Then Philip began with that very passage of Scripture and told him the good news about Jesus" (v. 35).

Philip understood that Jesus was the fulfillment of the Old Testament prophecies concerning the Lamb of God. Hopefully, we too will also be able to explain to others that Jesus is the "Lamb of God who takes away the sin of the world!"

A Heart of Flesh

So, why did God harden Pharaoh's heart? So that through the foreshadowing of Old Testament types, we might "Behold, the Lamb of God that takes away the sin of the world."

A hardened heart in medical terms is called a cardiomyopathy. Aside from a heart transplant, there is no cure for a cardiomyopathy. As a medical student rotating on the cardiology service, I became fond of a patient who was suffering from a cardiomyopathy. We became friends and shared dinner on several occasions in the hospital cafeteria. He lived in an apartment across the street from the hospital so he could be in close proximity in case a donor heart was found. I rotated off the cardiology service and missed seeing my friend for several months. One night I ran across his wife in the hospital and inquired about his well-being. I was saddened to learn he had passed away. No donor heart had been found in time.

To receive a heart transplant, the donor heart has to be a perfect match and the organ must be received before it's too late. The spiritual corollary to a cardiomyopathy is a "hardened heart." The only cure for a hardened heart is a spiritual heart transplant; we must find the perfect heart and receive the transplant before we run out of time. The heart transplant we need is the perfect heart of the Living Word—the Lamb of God. When we receive God's gift of salvation by receiving Christ as our Passover Lamb, He fulfills both roles of the sacrificial lamb and the scapegoat. Our sins are paid for and removed "as far as the east is from the west." Then we can claim God's promise: "I will give you a new heart and put a new spirit in you; I will remove from you your heart of stone and give you a heart of flesh" (Ezekiel 36:26).

— CHAPTER TWO QUESTIONS —

1. The author states, "God hardened Pharaoh's heart in order to reveal to us prophetic truths through the plagues He brought upon Egypt."
   a. What "prophetic truths" could God have revealed through each of the plagues on Egypt?
   b. What is the significance of the Passover plague's position as the last and final plague?

2. God promised that Sarah and Abraham would have a son, but he caused Sarah to wait until she was past the ability to give birth.
   a. Why do you suppose God made her wait so long?
   b. Could this be a foreshadowing of the birth of Christ?
   c. What other applications can be made concerning God's timing?

3. Explain how Isaac foreshadowed prophetic information about Christ through the following:
   a. His birth
   b. God's request for a sacrifice
   c. The three-day journey
   d. The location of the sacrifice
   e. Isaac carrying the wood to the place of sacrifice
   f. His willingness to be sacrificed
   g. The answer to Isaac's question, "but where is the lamb?"
   h. The ram with its head caught in the thorns
   i. The presence of the Angel of the Lord

4. Concerning the passage describing Cain and Abel, the author states: "It's no coincidence that this passage follows the 'fall of man.'" Why do you believe the author made that statement?

5. After rejecting Cain's offering, the Lord said to him: "If you do what is right, will you not be accepted?"

   a. What did the Lord mean by that statement?
   b. Does that statement apply to people living today?

6. The Last Supper was actually the Passover meal that Jesus commemorated with His disciples the night before He was crucified. Concerning that meal, Jesus requested that from then on the meal should be commemorated "in remembrance of me" (Luke 22:19). Explain how we can remember Jesus' fulfillment of the many aspects of Passover:

   a. Lamb selection day
   b. Sacrificial lamb
   c. Blood placed on the door post
   d. The unleavened bread
   e. The wine

SPIRITUAL SUSTENANCE

I tell you the truth, unless you eat the flesh of the Son of Man and drink his blood, you have no life in you. —John 6:53

Pernicious anemia is a gastrointestinal disorder that results in a deficiency of blood. The cause is the absence of a gastrointestinal substance called "intrinsic factor" that normally functions to allow the absorption of ingested vitamin B12, which is essential for the normal production of blood. A patient suffering from pernicious anemia can ingest adequate amounts of vitamin B12, but without the intrinsic factor, their body cannot absorb it. The result is anemia—a deficiency of blood.

The spiritual corollary is a condition I will call spiritual anemia. Spiritual anemia is an eternally fatal disorder of the soul that is also due, in a sense, to a deficiency of blood. Hebrews 9:22 explains, "without the shedding of blood there is no forgiveness." Therefore, to obtain God's forgiveness and become a part of the body of Christ—a Christian—blood is required.

The Israelites sacrificed an enormous amount of blood from innocent animals as a part of their religious ordinances; yet they failed to receive everlasting forgiveness. They were deficient in the blood necessary to be eternally forgiven of their sins. They suffered from spiritual anemia because they lacked the "spiritual intrinsic factor"!

The spiritual intrinsic factor needed to cure a person of spiritual anemia is the finished work of Jesus on the cross. The Law, with its sacrificial bloodshed of innocent animals, was a foreshadowing of

Christ's shed blood on the cross as the ultimate sacrifice for the forgiveness of sin. Romans 3:21-25 tells us,

> But now a righteousness from God, apart from law, has been known, *to which the Law and the Prophets testify*. This righteousness from God comes through faith in Jesus Christ to all who believe. There is no difference, for all have sinned and fall short of the glory of God, and are justified freely by his grace through the redemption that came by Christ Jesus. God presented him as a sacrifice of atonement, *through faith in his blood*. (emphasis added)

The Bread and the Wine

Jesus said, "unless you eat the flesh of the Son of Man and drink his blood, you have no life in you" (John 6:53). What did Jesus mean by eating His flesh and drinking His blood? This concept was difficult for the Jews to understand and it would become a stumbling block for them. "On hearing it, many of his disciples said, 'This is a hard teaching. Who can accept it?' ...From this time many of his disciples turned back and no longer followed him" (John 6:60, 66). This was not only a "hard teaching" for the Jews at that time, it would be a difficult concept for years to come.

Jesus was talking about a spiritual sustenance that we as the body of Christ would receive. He was not talking about His physical flesh and blood! This spiritual sustenance is the fulfillment to which "the Law and the Prophets testify."

Many throughout the ages have continued to be perplexed and confused by this teaching. For example, *The New Foxe's Book of Martyrs* describes the following incident:

> In 1532, Thomas Harding and his wife were accused of heresy because they denied that the bread and wine turned into the actual body and blood of Christ when the priest prayed over them in the mass. For this, the bishop of Lincoln, in eastern England, condemned them to be burned alive at the stake.[1]

Testimony of the Law and the Prophets

Let's take a look at the testimony of the Law and the Prophets. In the Law we read the account of the Exodus when the Israelites were freed from Egypt and journeyed through the wilderness. The journey of God's people is a symbolic foreshadowing of our spiritual journey.

When the Israelites were in bondage in Egypt, the event that allowed for their release was the last plague—the Passover Plague. We too are in bondage—a spiritual bondage to sin that results in spiritual death! And just as the Israelites were allowed to begin their journey of freedom because of the sacrifice of the Passover lamb, we too are freed from spiritual bondage by receiving Christ as our Passover Lamb.

When the Israelites left Egypt, they did not go directly to the Promised Land. They had to spend some time in the wilderness. Likewise, when we receive Christ as our Passover Lamb and begin our spiritual journey, we don't go immediately to our Promised Land—heaven! We spend some time in the wilderness of this world.

While the Israelites were in the wilderness, there was nothing there to sustain them. God provided for all of their needs, including their sustenance. He provided bread from heaven, called "manna," and "living water." In our spiritual journey, once we have been spiritually reborn there is nothing in this world that can sustain us spiritually. Christ provides our spiritual sustenance. Jesus said,

> I am the living bread that came down from heaven. If anyone eats of this bread, he will live forever. This bread is my flesh, which I will give for the life of the world …If anyone is thirsty, let him come to me and drink. Whoever believes in me, as the Scripture has said, streams of living water will flow from within him (John 6:51, 7:37-38).

Jesus is not only the fulfillment of the Passover that begins our spiritual journey, but also the spiritual food and drink that sustains us along the way.

The imagery of these prophecies was used again during the Last Supper—it occurred on the day of Passover. During that meal Jesus offered His disciples bread and the wine saying,

> "This is my body given for you; do this in remembrance of me ... This cup is the new covenant in my blood, which is poured out for you" (Luke 22:19-20).

Melchizedek Foreshadows Christ

The events of the Last Supper—the Messiah offering the symbolic bread and wine—were foreshadowed all the way back in the Book of Genesis. In Genesis 14 we are told that a coalition of four kings, led by Kedorlaomer, defeated the kings that ruled in the Valley of Siddim (the Salt Sea). They conquered the entire territory and seized their goods, including those of Sodom and Gomorrah. Genesis 14:12 tells us, "They also carried off Abram's nephew Lot and his possessions, since he was living in Sodom."

When Abram, who would later be called Abraham, heard that his relative had been taken captive, he pursued the allied kings with 318 trained men from his clan. He overtook the coalition, defeated them, and returned with Lot's household and all the plundered possessions! Here we see the obvious divine intervention of God, for how else could 318 men defeat the armies of four allied kings unless God had performed a great miracle? God's hand was clearly evident here!

When Abram returned, two kings met him in the Valley of Shaveh (the King's Valley): Melchizedek and the king of Sodom. Looking closely at this passage we find that both kings offered Abram something and Abram made a critical decision.

Concerning Melchizedek, we learn in the fourth verse of Psalm 110 that he was a type of Christ: "You are a priest forever, in the order of Melchizedek." The writer of Hebrews reiterates: "And what we have said is even more clear if another priest like Melchizedek appears, one who has become a priest not on the basis of a regulation as to his ancestry but on the basis of the power of an *indestructible life*" (Hebrews 7:15-16, emphasis added). In other words, another priest "like Melchizedek" appeared and arose from the dead, proving that His life was "indestructible." Jesus is the priest "in the order of Melchizedek." He is the fulfillment to which Melchizedek was pointing!

So what does "the order of Melchizedek" mean? According to Genesis 14:18, Melchizedek was the priest-king of Salem, a pagan Jebusite city. Salem was later renamed Jeru-salem and was eventually captured by David, who made it the capital of Judah (2 Samuel 5). Melchizedek was, therefore, a priest and king who ruled from Jerusalem.

In the Israelite legal system, the priests and the kings did not infringe on each other's duties—priests were not the rulers; kings didn't perform priestly sacrifices. The consequences of disobedience were serious! For example, King Uzziah was stricken with leprosy when he tried to perform the priestly duty of offering incense in the Temple (2 Chronicles 26).

The order of Melchizedek foreshadows for us that the Messiah would combine both offices; He would serve as king and priest. Further, the name Salem means "peace" and the name Melchizedek means "king of righteousness." Therefore, in Melchizedek we see a beautiful foreshadowing of Christ. He is our Great High Priest and our King of Kings! He is the Prince of Peace and the Lord our Righteousness! Furthermore, the Scriptures reveal that when Jesus comes back to earth to establish His throne during the millennial reign, it will be in the city of "the New Jerusalem" (Revelation 21).

Melchizedek was clearly a beautiful type of Christ. What did he offer to Abram? Bread and wine (Genesis 14:18)! Christ offered the same thing to his disciples at the Last Supper and explained to them the symbolic meaning: the bread represents His body, the wine His blood (Luke 22:19-20).

Melchizedek blessed Abram in the name of El Elyon, "God Most High," and praised God for giving Abram victory in battle. Abram then presented a tithe to Melchizedek indicating his recognition of Melchizedek as a fellow worshiper of the one true God and a priest who ranked higher (spiritually) than himself.

The Shadow of the Enemy

What about the king of Sodom? Both kings met Abram on his return and they both offered him something. If Melchizedek was a type of Christ, who did the king of Sodom represent?

Concerning Sodom, we are told in the previous chapter of Genesis: "Now the men of Sodom were wicked and were sinning greatly against the Lord" (Genesis 13:13). If Sodom represents the wickedness of this world, then the king of Sodom may represent the king of this world—Satan.

What did the king of Sodom offer Abram? Let's look at the dialogue between the two men: "The king of Sodom said to Abram, 'Give me the people and keep the goods for yourself'" (Genesis 14:21). He offered Abram nothing! On the surface it appears that he offered Abram the possessions but Abram already had them. In actuality, the king of Sodom offered Abram nothing!

So what did the king of Sodom want? He wanted the people! This is the same scheme that Satan uses today. He has nothing to offer anyone. Material possessions are only temporary; they are the wood, hay, and stubble that will be burned on the Day of Judgment (1 Corinthians 3:11-15). Satan seeks to distract people with materialism, the love of things; meanwhile he wants their souls! He wants to gather as many souls to himself as possible before the Second Coming of Christ.

Our proper response to Satan is scripted for us in this prophetic story. Genesis 14:22-23 tells us,

> But Abram said to the king of Sodom, "I have raised my hand to the Lord, God Most High, Creator of heaven and earth, and have taken an oath that I will accept nothing belonging to you, not even a thread or the thong of a sandal, so that you will never be able to say, 'I made Abram rich.'"

All people will at some time in their lives, probably multiple times, find themselves in Abram's position. We will be confronted with a choice between the two kings. One has nothing to offer and tries to distract us with materialism and things that are not lasting. He is the king of this world and he wants our souls! The other king offers us the symbolic meaning of the bread and the wine: forgiveness of sin and eternal life. He is the Prince of Peace and the King of Kings. What choice will we make? Abram chose the priest-king and became our father in the faith. Our eternal destiny depends upon our decision!

The Blessing of the Bread and Wine

The prophetic concept of the blessing of bread and wine is revealed further in Genesis 27. We already have discussed Isaac as a type Christ. He was the promised child, born through divine intervention, who carried the wood on his back to Mount Moriah (Calvary) for the sacrificial offering. Later in his life, as Isaac became an aged man, we see him employed as a type of Christ again.

Shortly before his death, Isaac called his eldest son Esau to his side so that he could bestow upon him the customary blessing of the birthright. The story takes an unexpected twist when Jacob, Esau's younger brother, tricks his blind father and receives the blessing instead!

When Esau arrives on the scene with some specially prepared game for his father, Isaac is shocked and remorseful as he tells him that he has already given the blessing to Jacob. Esau pleads with his father, "Haven't you reserved any blessing for me?" (Genesis 27:36). Isaac's answer is prophetic and echoes the meaning of Melchizedek's offering to Abram: "I have made him lord over you...and I have *sustained him with grain and new wine*" (Genesis 27:37, emphasis added). Again, an Old Testament character, a type of Christ, offers the blessing of the bread and wine—a foreshadowing of what Christ did at the Last Supper.

It is also significant that according to the mores of that time, Jacob did not deserve the blessing. He was not the firstborn, yet he brought the young goat to his father and received the inheritance. This is a parallel prophecy to the story of Cain and Abel. Abel was not the firstborn; yet he brought the offering of the "firstborn of the flock" and received God's blessing. The meaning for us is that although we don't deserve the blessing of God's inheritance, through the offering of the firstborn Lamb of God, we can receive that blessing and be sustained by the symbolic meaning of the bread and wine. We have the opportunity to become fellow heirs with Christ and receive eternal sustenance.

The Bread of Life

Let's take a closer look at our spiritual sustenance—the bread and the wine. In the sixth chapter of the Gospel of John, we read of the great miracle that Jesus performed when he fed the crowd of over 5000 with five small loaves of bread and two small fish. After feeding the multitude, Jesus and His disciples crossed the lake. The next day, some of the people who had eaten the loaves and fish followed Jesus to Capernaum and asked this question:

"What miraculous sign then will you give that we may see it and believe you?

What will you do? Our forefathers ate the manna in the desert; as it is written: 'He gave them bread from heaven to eat.'" (John 6:30)

Amazing! Jesus performed an incredible miracle by literally feeding thousands of people with five small loaves of bread and two small fish and they still didn't believe in Him! What miracle would convince them to believe? The Scriptures give us the answer:

> Jesus said to them, "I tell you the truth, it is not Moses who has given you the bread from heaven, but it is my Father who gives you the true bread from heaven. For the bread of God is he who comes down from heaven and gives life to the world." "Sir," they said, "from now on give us this bread." Then Jesus declared, "I am the bread of life. He who comes to me will never go hungry, and he who believes in me will never be thirsty." (John 6:30-35)

Jesus explained that the incredible miracle of the manna was a foreshadowing of Himself—the "true bread from heaven."

During the Exodus, the people came to an area called the "Desert of Sin" where they were hungry and without anything to eat. They began murmuring against God. He gave them the great miracle of the manna, which they called "bread from heaven." The Scriptures tell us, "It was white like coriander seed and tasted like wafers made with honey" (Exodus 16:31). It is estimated that 1,500 tons of manna would have been required each morning and twice that amount on the sixth morning, as they received a double portion on the day before the Sabbath. It has also been estimated that it would have taken two freight trains, each a mile-long, to hold the amount of manna required for just the daily provision! Amazingly enough, scientists have tried—without success—to identify any substance near the location of the Israelite's Exodus to match the characteristics of the manna.

Let's look at how the manna was symbolic of the Word of God. The manna was round, which is symbolic of being complete or eternal. Jesus said His Word is eternal, "Heaven and earth will pass away, but my words will never pass away" (Matthew 24:35). The manna was white, which is symbolic of purity or holiness. Likewise, the Scriptures testify, "The words of the Lord are flawless, like silver refined in a furnace of clay, purified seven times" (Psalm 12:6). Additionally, we are told the manna tasted like honey. In Revelation 10:10, the apostle John relates, "I took the little scroll from the angel's hand and ate it. It tasted sweet as honey." And so we see that the Word of God is the fulfillment of the manna. It is eternal, flawless, and sweet as honey!

When Jesus was tempted in the wilderness, we are told that He fasted for forty days and was hungry. "The tempter came to him and said, 'If you are the Son of God, tell these stones to become bread.' Jesus answered, 'It is written: "Man does not live on bread alone, but on every word that comes from the mouth of God"'" (Matthew 4:3-4). Jesus is telling us that our spiritual sustenance is the Word of God. The world is the wilderness of sin and it has nothing to sustain us spiritually. God has provided for our spiritual sustenance by supplying us with His Word.

To serve as a reminder of the great miracle of the manna, God commanded that a jar containing an omer of manna be placed in the Ark of the Covenant. The ark held only three items: the tablets of God's Word, the jar of manna, and Aaron's rod that budded (Numbers 17). All three foreshadowed different aspects of the One who eventually would become the Ark of the new covenant—Jesus Christ.

The tablets of God's Word and the manna, which was a type of the Word of God, foreshadowed Jesus Christ, the Living Word of God.

Aaron's rod was chosen from twelve rods, each representing a tribe of Israel. When Aaron's rod "not only sprouted but...budded, blossomed and produced almonds" (Numbers 17:8), it was a sign from the Lord that Aaron was indeed God's chosen high priest over His people. It was a foreshadowing of Jesus, the Chosen One, who is our Great High Priest. The dead rod's coming back to life and sprouting fruit was a type of the death and resurrection of Christ and the fruit of the Holy Spirit.

Jesus, the Living Word, is the fulfillment of the manna; He is the "true bread from Heaven." Like the Israelites, after we are freed from our bondage to sin by receiving Christ as our Passover Lamb, we begin our spiritual journey into the wilderness of this world. The world has nothing to sustain us spiritually. Jesus is our spiritual sustenance! "The Son is the radiance of God's glory and the exact representation of his being, *sustaining all things by his powerful word*" (Hebrews 1:3, emphasis added).

Significance of the Wine

As we discussed in chapter one, Jesus performed miracles constantly: "News about him spread all over Syria, and people brought to him *all* who were ill with various diseases, those suffering severe pain, the demon-possessed, those having seizures, and the paralyzed, and he healed them" (Matthew 4:24, emphasis added). As He went about His everyday activities, some individuals were healed simply by touching His garments (Luke 8:44).

We also established that only a small portion of Jesus' miracles actually was recorded in the Scriptures. God chose to record them for specific reasons. Realizing God's divine guidance in the recording of Jesus' miracles, one might suppose that His first recorded miracle would be of special significance.

The first of Jesus' recorded miracles is when He turned water into wine during a wedding feast at Cana (John 2:1-11). Why was this miracle selected? What was so significant about it that it became His first recorded miracle? Many have struggled to understand the meaning of this miracle. Why would Jesus turn water into wine? Why did He attend a wedding celebration?

In the Scriptures God sometimes uses seemingly insignificant details to teach us prophetic truths. The key to unlocking the mystery of this miracle's significance hinges on the kind of jars that were used. To overlook that fact is to miss the prophetic point that Jesus so beautifully makes through this miracle. We are told the jars were "the kind used by the Jews for ceremonial washing" (John 2:6). The Jews used these stone containers (each holding twenty to thirty gallons of water) to wash and make themselves ceremonial clean before God. The ceremonial cleansing was only temporary, however; it only cleansed the outside. To be forgiven of sin required the shedding of blood (Hebrews 9:22).

It was no coincidence that the jars Jesus selected were those used for ceremonial cleansing. At the Last Supper, Jesus explained that the wine represented His blood, which was shed for the forgiveness of our sins. "This cup is the new covenant in my blood, which is poured out for you" (Luke 22:20). Jesus came as the ultimate sacrifice and we are cleansed before God through faith in His blood. "How much more, then, will the blood of Christ, who through the eternal Spirit offered himself unblemished to God, cleanse our consciences from acts that lead to death" (Hebrews 9:14). Turning the water (used for ceremonial washing) into wine foreshadowed the symbolic meaning of Jesus' blood cleansing us from sin. Understanding this prophetic meaning helps us to better comprehend the rest of the passage.

The wedding feast at Cana was a foreshadowing of another wedding day when the Bridegroom, Jesus Christ, will come for His bride. The passage begins "On the third day a wedding took place" (John 2:1). But there is no tie to the previous passage, which leads us to ask, "On the third day of what?" Realizing the passage is prophecy, the third day foreshadows the resurrection of Jesus on the third day which allows Him to take His place as our Bridegroom. This explains why when Mary said, "They have no more wine," Jesus replied, "My time has not yet come" (John 2:3,4).

When the master of the banquet tasted the newly transformed wine, he proclaimed that the bridegroom had saved the best wine till last. This was a foreshadowing that the new covenant of Jesus' blood is better than the old covenant of the Law. The new covenant, represented by the wine, took the place of the old covenant, represented by the water in the ceremonial jars. The wine was a foreshadowing of the blood of Christ that was shed for the remission of our sins!

Jesus Christ — The Real Meaning of the Bread and the Wine

Year after year the Jews celebrate Passover by drinking wine (symbolic of our forgiveness of sins) and eating unleavened bread (symbolic of our spiritual sustenance). Even though they physically ingest these symbolic nutrients, they still suffer from spiritual anemia because they lack the intrinsic factor—the cross! Unless we accept the blood of Christ that was shed on the cross, we suffer from the eternally fatal disorder of spiritual anemia.

A priest-king, on the order of Melchizedek, has come and offered us the bread of sustenance and the wine of forgiveness through His finished work on the cross. He proved Himself on "the basis of the power of an indestructible life," (Hebrews 7:16) by His resurrection on the third day.

The Bridegroom is waiting and we have a choice to make. We can choose the Great High Priest and King of Kings or we can choose the king of this world. Our eternal destiny hangs in the balance of our choice!

— CHAPTER THREE QUESTIONS —

1. The author describes the Old Testament Jews as suffering from "spiritual anemia."
   a. What did he mean by that description?
   b. How could "spiritual anemia" describe someone today?
   c. Is there a difference between believing in Jesus and receiving Him as Savior? (Consider James 2:19)

2. Transubstantiation is the Catholic doctrine that the bread and wine (Eucharist) transforms into the actual flesh and blood of Jesus after the priests pray over it. It was for denying this doctrine that Thomas Harding and his wife were burned at the stake in A.D. 1532. Look at Paul's words in Romans 3:21-25.
   a. What does Paul mean by "faith in his blood"?
   b. Do you think that Paul was advocating actually drinking the blood of Christ?

3. Review John 6:25-64. Is Jesus advocating the consumption of His physical flesh and blood or symbolizing a spiritual truth? (Consider verse 63 as you determine your answer)

4. Explain how Melchizedek was a type of Christ: (Consider Genesis 14, Psalm 110:4, and Hebrews 7)
   a. The meaning of his name
   b. The meaning of his position
   c. The meaning of Salem
   d. The significance of ruling from Jerusalem
   e. The significance of the bread and the wine
   f. The significance of Abram's tithe
   g. The significance of Melchizedek's blessing

5. Review Genesis 14 and answer the following:
   a. If Melchizedek was intended by God to represent a foreshadowing of Christ, then whom does the king of Sodom represent?
   b. What does Abram's dialogue with the king of Sodom reveal to us about the desire of our adversary and our proper response?

6. Review Jesus' first recorded miracle in John 2:1-11. Explain the following:
   a. Why did Jesus select jars used for ceremonial washing instead of the customary wine jars?
   b. When confronted by Mary, why did Jesus reply, "My time has not yet come"?
   c. If the passage is prophecy, what do the clay jars represent? (Consider 2 Corinthians 4:7)
   d. What is the symbolic meaning of the wine?
   e. What is the significance of the occasion—a wedding banquet? (Consider Revelation 19:6-9)
   f. Who does the master of the banquet represent? (Consider Luke 14:15-24)
   g. What is the meaning of the master of the banquet's statement: "You have saved the best till now"?

— CHAPTER FOUR —

THE SPRING FEASTS

*These are my appointed feasts, the appointed feasts of the Lord,
which you are to proclaim as sacred assemblies. — Leviticus 23:2*

*A*cute epiglottitis can be an anesthesiologist's nightmare. Although easily treated with antibiotics, sometimes the epiglottis (usually protective of the opening of the windpipe) rapidly becomes so swollen and inflamed that it becomes an obstruction to the windpipe. Patients with acute epiglottitis exhibit a very characteristic appearance: they sit upright, leaning slightly forward; because they can't swallow saliva drools out of their mouth; their voice becomes markedly hoarse; and they have difficulty breathing.

To treat the severe case of acute epiglottitis, a breathing tube is placed into the patient's windpipe. This tube provides an open airway passage, while allowing the antibiotics time to work alleviating the epiglottic swelling. Anesthetizing someone in this severe condition is almost as frightening for the anesthesiologist as it is for the patient! Once the patient is anesthetized, there is only a brief window of time in which to accomplish the placement of the breathing tube. If anesthetized improperly, the swollen epiglottis can *itself* become an obstruction to the patient's windpipe, making the placement of a breathing tube extremely difficult, if not impossible. The critical nature of this situation is the realization that if the breathing tube cannot be placed, death may result in the span of only a few minutes! Thankfully, the proper technique for inducing anesthesia in this situation is well known and has been proven effective. A lack of knowledge about the proper treatment, however, can prove fatal!

This was evident in the death of our nation's first president George Washington. His last few days of life, as described in the biography written by Washington Irving, reveals that he developed an acute illness that progressed in a very characteristic manner resembling epiglottitis. He had just returned to his home at Mount Vernon. Irving writes:

> On the following morning the snow was three inches deep and still falling, which prevented him from taking his usual ride. He complained of a sore throat, and had evidently taken cold the day before...A hoarseness which had hung about him through the day grew worse towards the night but he made light of it.
>
> In the night he was taken extremely ill with ague and difficulty of breathing...Washington desired that Dr. Craik, who lived in Alexandria, should be sent for and that in the meantime Rawlins, one of the overseers, should be summoned to bleed him before the doctor could arrive.
>
> A gargle was prepared for his throat, but whenever he attempted to swallow any of it he was convulsed and almost suffocated. Rawlins made his appearance soon after sunrise but, when the general's arm was ready for the operation, became agitated.
>
> "Don't be afraid," said the general, as well as he could speak. Rawlins made an incision.
>
> "The orifice is not large enough," said Washington.
>
> The blood, however, ran pretty freely and Mrs. Washington, uncertain whether the treatment was proper and fearful that too much blood might be taken, begged Mr. Lear to stop it.
>
> When he was about to untie the string the general put up his hand to prevent him, and as soon as he could speak, murmured, "More...more."
>
> But Mrs. Washington's doubts prevailed, and the bleeding was stopped after about half a pint of blood had been taken.

His old friend, Dr. Craik, arrived between eight and nine, and two other physicians, Drs. Dick and Brown were called in. Various remedies were tried and additional bleeding, but all of no avail.

In the course of the afternoon he appeared to be in great pain and distress from the difficulty of breathing, and frequently changed his posture in the bed.

About ten minutes before he expired (which was between ten and eleven o'clock) his breathing became easier...Dr. Craik put his hands over his eyes and he expired without a struggle or a sigh.[1]

Two things are evident from George Washington's last moments, as recorded in his biography. First, the physicians of his day did not understand his illness or its proper treatment. And secondly, they practiced shedding blood without fully understanding what they were doing!

From this historical example, we can draw a spiritual analogy regarding the Israelites in the Old Testament. They did not understand their condition (spiritual anemia) or its proper cure. Their religious ceremonies (feasts) called for the shedding of blood. They dutifully participated in the shedding of blood of sacrificial animals without fully understanding the meaning behind what they were doing! Like those physicians treating George Washington, the Israelites didn't fully understand the reason why they were shedding blood or the cure for the illness that afflicted their people. And like the potentially deadly outcome of treating acute epiglottitis, a lack of spiritual understanding can prove fatal as well—eternally fatal!

The Seven Sacred Feasts

The Old Testament sacrificial system was punctuated by seven sacred feasts throughout the year. In order for us to understand the prophetic significance of what God was orchestrating through the sacrificial system, we need to take a close look at these seven annual feasts. In Leviticus 23, God gave Moses the details for the seven annual feasts. These seven sacred assemblies were observed annually for thousands of years. Speaking of the feasts, the apostle Paul tells us they were "a shadow of the things that were to come; the reality, however, is found in Christ" (Colossians 2:17). The feasts, Paul explains, were a foreshadowing of Christ. In other words, when God was providing the details of each of these feasts, He was also providing details about Christ!

Before examining each feast in-depth, we need a firm foundation upon which to build. First, these feasts are not merely Jewish feasts that are applicable only to the Hebrews. In Leviticus 23:1-2 we are told, "The Lord said to Moses, 'Speak to the Israelites and say to them: "These are my appointed feasts, the appointed *feasts of the Lord,* which you are to proclaim as sacred assemblies"'" (emphasis added). So these seven annual feasts are *"feasts of the Lord."* They are not Jewish feasts to be observed only by the Jews; they are God's feasts and their *message is for God's people.*

Secondly, these feasts are not banquets or festivals. They are *"sacred assemblies."* John Hagee writes, "The Hebrew word for feast, *mo'ed,* means 'a set or appointed time.' Of similar meaning is *mikrah,* indicating 'a rehearsal or recital.' Each feast, like a dress rehearsal, offers a significant picture of the future. The combined seven feasts are a divine blueprint of what lies ahead."[2] These feasts outline *acts of worship* that God ordained to be performed at appointed times in the calendar year for the purpose of revealing prophetic information about Christ.

Significance of the Spring and Fall

The feasts are clustered into two groups: spring feasts and fall feasts. God placed them in the spring and fall for a specific reason. The spring feasts center around the spring barley harvest; the fall feasts center around the fall wheat harvest. In the land of Palestine, there are two rainy seasons. The rains that provide for the spring barley harvest are known as the spring rains; the rains that provide for the fall wheat harvest are known as the winter rains. Thousands of years before the birth of Christ, the prophet Hosea prophesied concerning the Messiah: "He will come to us like the winter rains, like the spring rains that water the earth" (Hosea 6:3).

Hosea was providing prophetic information concerning the *two Advents of Christ*. Just as the two seasons of rain bring about the two harvest seasons, Christ would come *twice* to fulfill God's plans. The Spring Feasts foreshadow Christ's first Advent when He fulfilled His role as the suffering Savior. The Fall Feasts, as we shall later see, reveal information concerning what Christ will do when He returns to fulfill His Second Advent, as the King of Kings and Lord of Lords. James evidently understood the two rainy seasons as being a foreshadowing of the two Advents of Christ, "Be patient, then, brothers, until the Lord's coming. See how the farmer waits for the land to yield its valuable crop and how patient he is for the *autumn and spring rains*. You too, be patient and stand firm, because the Lord's coming is near" (James 5:7-8, emphasis added).

The calendar year is the prophetic time frame through which God chooses to illustrate information concerning another time frame. The shadow it describes is the time of the new covenant to which the prophet Jeremiah referred.

> "The time is coming," declares the Lord, "when I will make a new covenant with the house of Israel and with the house of Judah. It will not be like the covenant I made with their forefathers when I took them by the hand to lead them out of Egypt, because they broke my covenant, though I was a husband to them," declares the Lord. "This is the covenant I will make with the house of Israel after that time," declares the Lord. "I will put my law in their minds and write it on their hearts. I will be their God, and they will be my people." (Jeremiah 31:31-33)

By strategically positioning the feasts at their appointed times, God was telling us information about the new covenant time period. The new covenant *began* with Christ's first coming to the earth and it will *end* with His Second Coming. The new covenant time period is therefore bracketed by the two Advents of Christ.

It is no coincidence that God ordained that the first feast, Passover, should mark the first month of the calendar year. We are told in Exodus 12:2, "This month is to be for you...the first month of your year." (See Figure 1[3], page 80) By issuing that command, God was prophetically orchestrating for us His divine blueprint of the new covenant time period. Just as the year would start with Passover, the new covenant time period would commence with Christ's fulfillment of that first Passover.

Let's examine each of the Spring Feasts in detail, and search out what God is telling us concerning Christ's first Advent when He fulfilled His role as the suffering Savior.

Feast of Passover

We already have seen in the previous chapters the fulfillment of Christ as the Lamb of God. The annual Passover Feast was a reminder that redemption comes by the blood of the lamb and prophetically pointed toward Jesus, who would one day be provided as the ultimate sacrificial lamb. The Passover lamb is the *preeminent type* upon which all the other types serve to provide additional information.

> Tell the whole community of Israel that on the tenth day of this month each man is to take a lamb for his family, one for each household...The animals you choose must be year-old males without defect, and you may take them from the sheep or the goats. Take care of them until the fourteenth day of the month, when all the people of the community of Israel must slaughter them at twilight. Then they are to take some of the blood and put it on the sides and tops of the doorframes of the houses where they eat the lambs. That same night they are to eat the meat roasted over the fire, along with bitter herbs, and bread made without yeast. (Exodus 12:2-3, 5-8)

As already discussed, when Paul wrote, "Christ died for our sins according to the Scriptures" (1 Corinthians 15:3), he was referring to the Old Testament Scriptures. He could not have been referring to the Gospels because they were not yet written. Nowhere in the

Old Testament Scriptures is the death of Christ better foretold than in the foreshadowing of the Passover lamb!

In the New Testament Scriptures, John the Baptist hailed Jesus as "the Lamb of God, who takes away the sin of the world" (John 1:29). Also, in the Book of Revelation, John the Revelator writes, "Then I saw a Lamb, looking as if it had been slain, standing in the center of the throne...He came and took the scroll from the right hand of him who sat on the throne. And when he had taken it, the four living creatures and the twenty-four elders fell down before the Lamb" (Revelation 5:6-8). He later reveals, "Then the angel said to me, 'Write: "Blessed are those who are invited to the wedding supper of the Lamb!"'" (Revelation 19:9). Jesus represented by the sacrificial lamb is the focal point of the Scriptures.

Ada Habershon, in his book *Study of the Types*, explains the importance of the description of the Passover, as recorded in the Book of Exodus.

> It tells of redemption by blood, the only means of deliverance from wrath; and it speaks to us of the need of personal appropriation, for there is not only the shed blood, but the sprinkled blood. The lamb must not only be slain for all Israel, but the blood must be poured into a basin and sprinkled on the doorposts and lintel, for the firstborn of each individual family.
>
> There are many people who believe in the shedding of the blood; they believe that the Lord Jesus died, but they have not appropriated His work for themselves, and so are not resting under the sprinkled blood. To have rested only on the fact that the lamb had been killed would not have brought safety; but having done what God had told them, the children of Israel were safe. Nothing but the blood could keep out the destroying angel; the strongest buildings in the land are specifically mentioned, but neither the throne nor the dungeon were secure—neither

palace guards nor prison walls could ensure safety. We read that "there was not a house where there was not one dead"; and though reference is made primarily to the houses of the Egyptians, it was true throughout the whole land, in the houses of the Israelites as well; for in each home there must be death—either of the firstborn or of the lamb.[4]

Jesus observed the Passover Feast as one of His final events before His arrest in the Garden of Gethsemane. In the book *The Feasts of the Lord,* Kevin Howard and Marvin Rosenthal provide insight into how the Feast of Passover was observed: "Several centuries before Christ, a somewhat traditionalized Passover service began to emerge. This ritual Passover service was called the *Seder* (pronounced SAY-der) from the Hebrew word meaning 'order.' It prescribed the traditional order of Scripture readings, prayers, symbolic foods, and songs in the Passover service."[5] Jesus not only fulfilled His role as the Passover Lamb, but also fulfilled the many aspects of the Passover Seder.

Howard and Rosenthal go on to explain that four glasses of wine were taken during the Passover service to symbolize the Lord's fourfold promise to deliver His people from Egypt:

> The Lord used four expressions to describe His promised deliverance from Egypt: "I will bring you out"; "I will rescue you from their bondage"; "I will redeem you"; and "I will take you as My people" (Exodus 6:6-7). Since wine is often a symbol of the joy of harvest, four cups of wine are taken during the Passover service to reflect the fourfold joy of the Lord's redemption.
>
> To begin the service, the father pours the first cup of wine and asks everyone to rise from the table. The father then lifts the cup of wine toward heaven and recites the *Kiddush* ("prayer of sanctification") to set the day apart to God."
>
> It was the Messiah, as the leader of the Seder service observed in the Upper Room, who said the Kiddush. "Then He took the cup, and gave thanks" (Luke 22:17).

The second ceremony of the Seder is known as the "washing of the hands." One of the family members brings a pitcher of water, bowl, and towel to each person at the table so that they may wash their hands. The ceremony was a symbolic act of purification as they prepare to handle the symbolic food.

It was probably this ceremony in the Seder that the Messiah used to teach His disciples an object lesson. "[Jesus] rose from supper and laid aside His garments, took a towel and girded Himself. After that, He poured water into a basin and began to wash the disciples' feet, and to wipe them with the towel with which He was girded." (John 13:4-5)[6]

This explains Peter's response when it came his turn to be washed: "Lord, are you going to wash my feet?" (John 13:6). The usual custom was to allow those present to wash their own hands; but Jesus was personally washing not their hands, but their feet. Jesus was teaching them several things by this act. First, He was giving them a practical example of His teaching in Matthew 20:26-28: "Whoever wants to become great among you must be your servant, and whoever wants to be first must be your slave—just as the Son of Man did not come to be served, but to serve, and to give his life as a ransom for many." He was also demonstrating to them the true meaning of this symbolic act of purification. It is Christ that cleanses and purifies us. Only the blood of the Lamb can truly cleanse us!

The next order of service was the dipping of a green vegetable into salt water. This was a reminder of the tears and suffering of the Israelites during their bondage.

Howard and Rosenthal explain further: "Before the second cup of wine is taken, the first half of the praise psalms, known in Judaism as the *Hallel* (Psalms 113—118), is recited responsively. *Hallel* is a Hebrew word meaning "praise." This word has made its way into many languages in the form of *hallelujah,* meaning "praise Jehovah."[7] Then the story of the ten plagues on Egypt is retold; with each plague, a little more wine was poured into the cup. After the conclusion of all ten plagues, the second cup of wine is taken, which commemorated the second promise of deliverance: "I will rescue you from their bondage."

Next a piece of *matzah* (unleavened bread) was dipped into a sweet sauce, which commemorated the sweetness of God's redemption in the midst of slavery. This is probably the time in the ceremony when Jesus exposed His betrayer. In John 13:21-26 we read:

> After he had said this, Jesus was troubled in spirit and testified, "I tell you the truth, one of you is going to betray me." His disciples stared at one another, at a loss to know which of them he meant. One of them, the disciple whom Jesus loved, was reclining next to him. Simon Peter motioned to this disciple and said, "Ask him which one he means." Leaning back against Jesus, he asked him, "Lord, who is it?" Jesus answered, "It is the one to whom I will give this piece of bread when I have dipped it in the dish." Then, dipping the piece of bread, he gave it to Judas Iscariot, son of Simon.

The next order of service was to eat the meal consisting of roasted lamb and unleavened bread. As we already have discussed, Jesus is the fulfillment of the Passover lamb and the unleavened bread.

After the meal, the third cup of wine was taken. The third cup was known as the "Cup of Redemption." It was a reminder of the third promise of deliverance: "I will redeem you." It was at this point that Jesus gave the true meaning of the unleavened bread and the third cup of wine. Howard and Rosenthal explain: "Luke reveals that it was "the cup after supper" (Luke 22:20), the third cup or the *Cup of Redemption,* that Jesus chose to be a reminder of His work on the cross."[8] Luke writes, "And he took bread, gave thanks and broke it, and gave it to them, saying, 'This is my body given for you; do this in remembrance of me.' In the same way, *after the supper* he took the cup, saying, 'This cup is the new covenant in my blood, which is poured out for you'" (Luke 22:19-20, emphasis added). Jesus was explaining to His disciples that He is the fulfillment of the symbolic meaning behind the unleavened bread and the cup of redemption.

The service traditionally draws to a close by taking the last cup of wine and singing the latter half of the Hallel psalms. The last cup of wine symbolized the fourth promise of deliverance: "I will take you as my people." The fulfillment of the last promise was dependent upon the previous promises. We cannot be God's people until the blood of the Lamb redeems us.

Taking a close look at the events of the Last Supper, we find an interesting detail concerning Jesus' observance of that particular Seder. Since Jesus had not yet gone to the cross to fulfill the meaning of the third cup, He refused to partake of the fourth cup! After taking the third cup, Jesus said, "'I tell you, I will not drink of this fruit of the vine from now on until that day when I drink it anew with you in my Father's kingdom.' When they had sung a hymn, they went out to the Mount of Olives" (Matthew 26:29-30).

In the garden, we are told that Jesus was, "overwhelmed with sorrow to the point of death," He prayed, "My Father, if it is possible, may this cup be taken from me. Yet not as I will, but as you will" (Matthew 26:38, 39). *This cup* to which He referred was the third cup; and as Jesus had just explained, it represented the shedding of His blood that would become the new covenant by which we are redeemed!

In summary, the Passover Feast reveals to us that we have redemption by the blood of the Lamb of God. Paul reminds us that "Christ, our *Passover lamb*, has been sacrificed" (1 Corinthians 5:7, emphasis added). When we receive Christ as our personal Passover Lamb, we become like those Israelite dwellings in Egypt, sealed by the blood of the Lamb. Alfred Edersheim makes an excellent observation concerning this concept:

> A most significant allusion to the typical meaning of the Passover blood, as a securing immunity from destruction, occurs in the prophecies of Ezekiel (Ezekiel 9:4-6), where "the man clothed with linen" is directed to "set a mark upon the foreheads" of the godly (like the first Passover—mark), so that they who were to "slay utterly old and young" might not "come near any" of them. The same symbolic reference and

command occur in the book of Revelation (Revelation 7:2-3; 9:4), in regard to those who have been "sealed as the servants of our God in their foreheads."[9]

C. H. Spurgeon elaborates further concerning the price of the Lamb of God that was paid for our redemption:

> In the Old Testament, one of the most instructive types of redemption ever given is that of the Passover lamb...What is expressly said by God Himself about this passing over? Hear the words, and wonderingly drink in their teaching! "And when I see the blood, I will pass over you." There was never a fuller type of the redemption of Christ, I hardly think one so full, as that of the passing - over is displayed to us in this sentence: "When I see the blood, I will pass over you." God's eye resting upon the evidence of a life having been taken instead of the sinner's life, is the reason why He passes over the sinner, so that he does not die.[10]

So we see how Christ perfectly fulfilled His role as the Passover lamb and provided our redemption! Redemption through the blood of the Lamb; it is what we sing about:

> *Redeemed, how I love to proclaim it:*
> *Redeemed by the blood of the Lamb;*
> *Redeemed through His infinite mercy,*
> *His child and forever I am.*[11]

Feast of Unleavened Bread

As the sun was setting on Nisan 15, the Feast of Passover drew to a close and the Feast of Unleavened Bread began. The Feast of Unleavened Bread was a seven-day feast, during which no leaven (yeast) was allowed. It wasn't sufficient to merely avoid yeast in their bread; the Israelites were commanded to avoid any yeast. We are told in Exodus 12:19: "For seven days no yeast is to be found in your houses." However, the command to avoid yeast went even further and applied to all areas of life, throughout their entire country! Exodus 13:7 further reveals, "Eat unleavened bread during those seven days; nothing with yeast in it is to be seen among you, nor shall any yeast be seen anywhere within your borders." Howard and Rosenthal explain:

> The clarity of God's command allows no room for debate. Any leaven, no matter how small the amount or how discreet its presence, is not permitted during the Feast of Unleavened Bread. It is not enough to simply refrain from eating leaven, or from touching leaven, or even from looking at leaven by storing it away in a hidden place. All leaven must be purged out. Failure to do so is a serious breech of biblical law.[12]

Indeed the penalty for breaching this command was severe. Exodus 12:19 informs us, "And whoever eats anything with yeast in it must be *cut off* from the community of Israel" (emphasis added).

The emphasis during this seven-day feast was not on the bread, but on the leaven. John Hagee points out:

> In the Bible, leaven is the type, or metaphor, for sin. Leaven represents the pride and arrogance that lead men to feel they have no need for God. Jesus said, "Take heed and beware of the leaven of the Pharisees and the Sadducees" (Matthew 16:6), and Paul added, "Your glorying is not good. Do you not know that a little leaven leavens the whole lump?" (1 Corinthians 5:6) The message of this feast? God has a zero tolerance for sin. Just like yeast, sin puffs us up. The Bible warns that our sins will find us out, and the wages of sin is death.[13]

For the Israelites, the unleavened bread was known as the "bread of affliction." It was a reminder of that night after the Passover when they left Egypt in haste, without time to allow the dough to rise. Deuteronomy 16:3 tells us, "For seven days eat unleavened bread, the bread of affliction, because you left Egypt in haste—so that all the days of your life you may remember the time of your departure from Egypt."

Grant Jeffrey adds:

> This unpleasant tasting bread symbolized all the burden and affliction in Egypt. Once Israel was free, this bread served as a reminder of the leaven and sinfulness of pagan Egypt that they had left behind, as well as the freedom they now enjoyed. The transformation of a symbol of bondage into one of freedom is paralleled for Christians in the transformation of the cross from a tragic symbol of death into the glorious reminder of Christ's victorious resurrection over death and the grave.[14]

Jesus is the fulfillment of the unleavened bread. As Grant Jeffrey further explains:

> Jesus described Himself by saying, "I am the bread of life" (John 6:35). Much of His ministry centered around the image of bread. Even Bethlehem, where He was born, means the "house of bread" in Hebrew. One time, when Jesus was talking to his disciples, He said: "The hour is come, that the Son of man should be glorified. Verily, verily, I say unto you, Except a corn of wheat fall into the ground and die, it abideth alone: but if it die, it bringeth forth much fruit..." (John 12:23).
>
> Christ the kernel of wheat (the basis for bread) did indeed have to die and be buried in a tomb on the Feast of Unleavened Bread, the fifteenth day of Nisan.[15]

So far we have seen that Jesus was crucified (and His blood shed) on the day of the Feast of Passover—*in fulfillment of His role as the Passover Lamb*. Because of that, we have redemption. Now we see that Jesus was buried on the Feast of Unleavened Bread—*in fulfillment of his role as unleavened bread—the absence of sin!*

The meaning for us—we too have become as unleavened bread! In dying for the forgiveness of our sins, *Jesus allows us to change places with Him.* We are informed in 2 Corinthians 5:21, "God made him who had no sin to be sin for us, so that in him we might become the righteousness of God."

We are further instructed by the apostle Paul, "Get rid of the old yeast that you may be a new batch without yeast—as you really are. For Christ, our Passover Lamb, has been sacrificed" (1 Corinthians 5:7). In other words, when we have received Christ as our personal Passover Lamb, we become a *"new batch without yeast."* Our sins are removed!

And finally, the duration of the Feast of Unleavened Bread is significant as well. It is a seven-day feast. Howard and Rosenthal explain that, "Seven is the biblical number for perfection and completeness"[16] The Feast of Unleavened Bread, therefore, foreshadows for us that in Christ we have the *complete* forgiveness of our sins!

Feast of Firstfruits

Some of the feasts make a transition straight from one feast into the next. The Feast of Passover becomes the Feast of Unleavened bread at dusk on Nisan 15, and the Feast of Unleavened Bread transitions into the Feast of Firstfruits on Nisan 16. Since the Feast of Unleavened Bread is a seven-day feast, the 16th of Nisan actually contains two feasts simultaneously—Unleavened Bread and Firstfruits.

The first day of the Feast of Unleavened Bread was a special Sabbath. "On the first day [of the Feast of Unleavened Bread] hold a sacred assembly and do no regular work" (Leviticus 23:7). We are told in Leviticus 23:9-11,14:

> The Lord said to Moses, "Speak to the Israelites and say to them: 'When you enter the land I am going to give you and you reap its harvest, bring to the priest a sheaf of the first [fruits] you harvest. He is to wave the sheaf before the Lord so it will be accepted on your behalf; the priest is to wave it on the day after the Sabbath....This is to be a lasting ordinance for the generations to come, wherever you live.'"

Historically for the Jews, the Feast of Firstfruits represents the crossing of the Red Sea after they were freed from Egyptian slavery. John Hagee writes, "The Feast of Firstfruits commemorates the day Israel went down into the depths of the Red Sea and came out the other side alive. The children of Israel marched into a watery grave and God received them on the other bank a nation of free people."[17] We see in the crossing of the Red Sea a very important spiritual principle: the salvation of God's people and *the destruction of those who were against God.*

This same principle was illustrated by the account of the Great Flood. Grant Jeffrey writes: "For a year Noah and his family floated upon the waters, no doubt wondering if they would ever see land or vegetation again. Imagine their gratitude to God when they felt their great ship rest on solid rock after nearly a year of not knowing when they would walk again upon the earth...One can easily imagine the descendants of Noah celebrating for many generations on this day, the "firstfruits" of their ultimate safe landing on the hills of the Earth."[18]

What this means is that when we become God's people (by receiving redemption through Christ's fulfillment of the Feast of Passover), we not only receive the forgiveness of sin (Feast of Unleavened Bread), but also eternal life. Howard and Rosenthal explain,

> Like Israel's other spring feasts, the Feast of Firstfruits found it's prophetic fulfillment in the work of Messiah's first coming. Paul declared..."But now Christ is risen from the dead, and has become the firstfruits of those who have fallen asleep" (1 Corinthians 15:20).
>
> But how was the Messiah our firstfruits? Jesus rose again on the third day (literally, the third day of Passover season, Nisan 16), on the day of the Firstfruits. But His resurrection had far greater implications. Paul explained, "For as in Adam all die, even so in Christ all shall be made alive" (1 Corinthians 15:22). The resurrection of Jesus is the guarantee and the beginning (firstfruits) of the final

harvest, or resurrection, of all mankind. The Messiah fulfilled the prophetic meaning of the holy day by rising from the dead to become the firstfruits of the resurrection, and He did it on the very day of Firstfruits.[19]

Feast of Pentecost
(Shavout, Feast of Weeks)

The fourth of the spring feasts was the Feast of Shavout, which means the "Feast of Weeks." The name came from the counting of fifty days (seven weeks) after the Feast of Firstfruits. The Greek word for the feast is *Pentecost*, meaning "fiftieth." Deuteronomy 16:10-12 gives three requirements for observing this feast:

> Then celebrate the Feast of Weeks to the Lord your God by giving a freewill offering in proportion to the blessings the Lord your God has given you. And rejoice before the Lord your God at the place he will choose as a dwelling for his Name—you, your sons and daughters, your menservants and maidservants, the Levites in your towns, and the aliens, the fatherless and the widows living among you. Remember that you were slaves in Egypt, and follow carefully these decrees.

In summary, the Israelites were to do three specific things: give back to the Lord in proportion to their blessings, rejoice wherever He chooses to dwell, and remember their release from bondage. These three mandates are even more meaningful when we understand the fulfillment of this feast.

The Giving of the Law

The Jews commemorate the Zeman Matan Tortenu, the "giving of the Law," at the Feast of Pentecost. Hagee writes,

> Following the Exodus and the Hebrews' miraculous escape from the Red Sea where the Israelites traveled until they reached the foothills of Mount Sinai, God instructed Moses to have the people purify themselves.

> At the end of their forty-seven-day journey, they
> purified themselves for three days, resulting in a
> total of fifty days, hence the word *pentecost.* Fearfully
> and faithfully they approached Mount Sinai, the
> great mountain of God, to receive the Ten
> Commandments.[20]

We read in Exodus 19 concerning the "giving of the Law," that on
the third morning there was the sound of a strong wind resembling
a trumpet blast. We're told "Mount Sinai was covered with smoke,
because the Lord descended on it in fire" (Exodus 19:18). We find a
similarity recorded in Acts 2 regarding the giving of the Holy Spirit.
On that Feast of Pentecost, the disciples heard "the blowing of a vio-
lent wind" (verse 2) from heaven; then they saw the Holy Spirit
descend on them as fire. Grant Jeffrey writes:

> It is no coincidence that on the same day of Pentecost
> in which God appeared to Moses in the wilderness of
> Sinai and revealed to man a new relationship based
> upon His sacred Law, He again revealed to man a new
> relationship based on His gift of the Holy Spirit. The
> mystical union of God and Israel that occurred on the
> Feast of Pentecost at the foot of Mount Sinai is mir-
> rored in the union of God's Holy Spirit with Christ's
> Bride, the Church, on Pentecost, fifty days after Christ
> rose from the dead.[21]

It is also interesting to note that the three days of purification prior
to the giving of the Law are an apparent foreshadowing for the three
days between the death and resurrection of Christ. Christ's sacrificial
death and subsequent resurrection is the basis of our spiritual purification and allows us to receive the gift of the Holy Spirit.

The Law Set Aside

As the Lord was giving Moses the details for observing the Feast
of Weeks, He included, "When you reap the harvest of your land, do
not reap to the very edges of your field or gather the gleanings of

your harvest. Leave them for the poor and the alien" (Leviticus 23:22). Jeffrey further points out:

> The Book of Ruth, which describes Boaz ordering his servants to leave the gleaning of the harvest for Ruth and her mother, is read in synagogues worldwide on the day of Pentecost. This harvest-time story records Ruth's conversion to Judaism: "And Ruth said, Entreat me not to leave thee, or to return from following after thee: for whither thou goest, I will go; and where thou lodgest, I will lodge: Thy people shall be my people, and thy God my God" (Ruth 1:16). The book ends with the genealogy of Ruth, showing that King David and, therefore, Jesus Christ, "the son of David," are descended from Ruth and Boaz (see Matthew 1:5-6).[22]

The Jews read the story of Ruth on the day of Pentecost each year, but they miss the beautiful foreshadowing that God gives through His Word! Boaz, the "kinsman –redeemer," foreshadows Christ—our spiritual kinsman-redeemer. Ruth was a Gentile. The Law forbade the Jews from intermarrying with the Gentiles; but we see that Boaz put away the Law to take Ruth as his bride. And as Jeffrey pointed out, Jesus of Nazareth, son of Joseph, became a descendant of the union between Boaz and his Gentile bride!

Christ also put away the Law and took to Himself His Gentile bride—the Church! This ushered in the new covenant, which includes the writing of the Law on our hearts by means of the Holy Spirit. When we accept Christ as our Savior and receive His Holy Spirit, we become the Gentile Bride of Christ.

The fulfillment of the Feast of Pentecost is the giving of the Holy Spirit. Once we understand that, we can fully understand the meaning behind the three mandates of Pentecost (as detailed in Deuteronomy 16).

First, we are to give an offering to God in proportion to our blessings. Our spiritual gifts are not to be hidden under a rock, but given back to the Lord through service that furthers His kingdom.

Second, we are to rejoice in the place God has chosen as a dwelling for His name. Notice that this command was not only for the Jews but for the "aliens" as well. The type here is the temple, God's old covenant dwelling place. The "antitype" (fulfillment) is our bodies—God's new covenant temple. He has chosen us as a dwelling place for His Holy Spirit!

Lastly, they were to remember their release from bondage. Likewise, we are to remember our release from bondage to sin and the forgiveness we receive through Christ.

The Spring Feasts Fulfilled

The physicians in George Washington's day did not understand the illness from which he suffered or its proper treatment. Additionally, they practiced the shedding of blood without understanding what they were doing. Likewise, the Israelites that we read about in the Old Testament did not understand the spiritual illness from which they were suffering or its proper treatment. They also dutifully carried out the sacrificial shedding of blood required by the ordinances that accompanied the Spring Feasts, without fully understanding the true meaning behind what they were doing.

The feasts were prophecies that pointed to the promised Messiah and what He would do on this earth. The Spring Feasts foreshadow for us in great detail what Jesus Christ fulfilled through His first Advent. Through His fulfillment of Passover, we have redemption—Christ paid the price as the sacrificial Lamb to redeem us. Through His fulfillment of Unleavened Bread, we have atonement—we are covered with the blood of the Lamb and appear as unleavened bread, without sin. Through His fulfillment of Firstfruits, we have eternal life—He arose as the firstfruits of those who will follow Him. Just as He arose from the dead, we too shall one day rise in a glorified body. And through His fulfillment of Pentecost, we have the gift of the Holy Spirit.

Jesus magnificently fulfilled the prophetic meanings of each of the Spring Feasts, and He accomplished them on the very day upon which each feast occurred! (See Figures 1 and 2 on pages 80-81.)

We, like the Israelites, are afflicted by a spiritual illness. Our Heavenly Father, the Great Physician, understands both our illness and its cure. We are suffering from a terminal illness called spiritual anemia. We all have sinned and fall short of the glory of God. We desperately need the cure of forgiveness; yet "without the shedding of blood there is no forgiveness" (Hebrews 9:22).

But as in the case of George Washington, it is not our blood that needs to be shed. When you are anemic, you require a blood transfusion. To be cured of our spiritual anemia, we need a spiritual blood transfusion; but before blood can be transfused, it has to be perfectly cross-matched. As Jesus went to the cross and shed His blood, God provided the perfect "cross"-matched blood that can cure us of our spiritual anemia forever!

God said through His prophet Isaiah, "I have no pleasure in the blood of bulls and lambs and goats" (Isaiah 1:11). All of the sacrificial blood shed during the Feasts of the Lord was pointing to the blood that can cure us of our spiritual illness. It was foreshadowing the blood of Christ that God would graciously provide. The apostle Paul explains: "But now in Christ Jesus you who once were far away have been brought near *through the blood of Christ*" (Ephesians 2:13, emphasis added).

Figure 1

NEW COVENANT TIME FRAME[3]

Calendar Year	January	February	March	April	May	June	July	August	September	October	November	December
Jewish Equivalent	Shevat	Adar	Nisan	Iyyar	Sivan	Tammuz	Av	Elul	Tishri	Cheshyan	Kislev	Tevet
Calendar as changed by God: (Begins with Nisan, which contains the Passover)	Nisan	Iyyar	Sivan	Tammuz	Av	Elul	Tishri	Cheshyan	Kislev	Tevet	Shevat	Adar

Nisan – *"This month is to be for you the first month." (Exodus 12:2)*

SEASONS

Spring ("spring rains")
  Nisan 14 — Passover
  Nisan 15-21 — Unleavened Bread
  Nisan 16 — Firstfruits
  Sivan 6 — Pentecost

FALL ("autumn rains")
  Tishri 1 — Trumpets
  Tishri 10 — Day of Atonement
  Tishri 15 — Tabernacles

"Be patient, then, brothers, until the Lord's coming. See how the farmer waits for the land to yield its valuable crop and how patient he is for the autumn and spring rains. You too, be patient and stand firm, because the Lord's coming is near." (James 5:7-8)

Figure 2

CHRIST'S FULFILLMENT OF THE SPRING FEASTS

Feast:	Event:	Significance:
Nisan 14 – Passover	Christ was crucified as the Lamb of God	We are redeemed
Nisan 15 – Unleavened Bread	Christ was buried	Our sins are buried
Nisan 16 – Firstfruits	Christ arose from the grave	We have eternal life
Sivan 6 – Pentecost	The Holy Spirit descended	Indwelling of the Holy Spirit

"These are a shadow of the things that were to come; the reality, however, is found in Christ."
(Colossians 2:17)

— CHAPTER FOUR QUESTIONS —

1. Concerning the Old Testament sacrificial system, the author states: "the Israelites didn't fully understand the reason why they were shedding blood."
   a. What was the meaning behind the practice of sacrifice?
   b. Should the Israelites have expected their Messiah to become a sacrifice? Explain your answer.

2. Writing to the Colossians, Paul said that the feasts were: "a shadow of the things that were to come; the reality, however, is found in Christ" (Colossians 2:17).
   a. What did Paul mean by that statement?
   b. How were the feasts a foreshadowing of Christ?

3. Concerning the Feast of Passover, how did Jesus fulfill the many aspects of this feast?
   a. Passover month beginning the calendar year
   b. Paschal lamb
   c. Unleavened bread
   d. Four cups of wine
   e. Cleansing ceremony
   f. The day that Jesus was crucified

4. Realizing that the Last Supper was Jesus' final observance of the Passover Seder with His disciples, what did He mean by His statement: "do this in remembrance of me" (Luke 22:19)?

5. Consider the Feast of Unleavened Bread:
   a. How was Jesus the fulfillment of this feast?
   b. What is the symbolic significance of unleavened bread? (See Matthew 16:6; 1 Corinthians 5:6)
   c. How does Jesus' fulfillment of this feast apply to us as Christians?

6. Realizing that Christ's resurrection took place on the day of the Feast of Firstfruits,

    a. What message is Paul trying to get across in his statement contained in 1 Corinthians 15:20?

    b. How does Christ's fulfillment of this feast apply to us as Christians?

7. At Pentecost, the Jews celebrate the "giving of the Law."

    a. What was given on the first Pentecost after the death of Jesus?

    b. Review Acts 2 and Exodus 19. How were the events that occurred similar?

    c. How does the fulfillment of the Feast of Pentecost relate to Jeremiah 31:33?

THE FALL FEASTS

Therefore do not let anyone judge you by what you eat or drink, or with regard to a religious [feast]...These are a shadow of the things that are to come; the reality, however, is found in Christ.
—*Colossians 2:16-17*

*I*n America in the 1950s, summertime was a time of fear and anxiety for many parents, this was the season when children by the thousands became infected with the crippling disease poliomyelitis, or polio. This burden of fear was lifted forever when it was announced that Dr. Jonas Salk had developed a vaccine against the disease...Salk's vaccine was composed of a "killed" polio virus, which retained the ability to immunize, without the risk of infecting the patient."[1]

How amazing that the product of something that was "killed," when injected into someone, could provide protection against a horrible illness that they would be exposed to in the future! The discovery of the polio vaccine has truly brought peace of mind and joy to humankind.

But, as horrible as polio may be, it pales in comparison to the "eternal illness" to which many will be exposed in the future. Likewise, we need not live in fear of this illness. We too may live with the peace of mind that someone has provided a killed vaccine. Jesus Christ, in fulfilling the meaning of the Spring Feasts, has become the killed vaccine for our sakes. The product of His death was the vaccination of the Holy Spirit that we receive upon accepting His gift of salvation. The Holy Spirit then makes us immune to the spiritual illness of eternal death.

The Fall Feasts foreshadow the time of Jesus' Second Coming when God's wrath will be poured out on those who have rejected His gift of salvation. They will suffer for an eternity in a state of spiritual death. Only those who have received the immunization of the Holy Spirit will be spared. Let's take a closer look at the Fall Feasts and how they foreshadow the Second Coming of Christ.

Feast of Trumpets
(Rosh Hashanah)

The Feast of Trumpets is the first of the three Fall Feasts:

> On the first day of the seventh month you are to have a day of rest, a sacred assembly commemorated with trumpet blasts (Leviticus 23:24).

All three Fall Feasts occur during the seventh Hebrew month—Tishri. Mitch and Zhava Glaser, in the book *The Fall Feasts of Israel*, point out:

> The number seven, symbolizing divine perfection, is woven into the entire Hebrew calendar. The Sabbath is observed on the seventh day of the week, every seventh year is decreed a sabbatical year, and after seven sabbatical years a Jubilee year is observed. Seven weeks after Passover comes the celebration of the Feast of Pentecost.
>
> Tishri is the sabbatical month and, along with the seventh day of the week, was set apart as sacred. So the seventh month is the most holy of months.[2]

Just as the Israelites went to God's dwelling place, the temple, to worship Him on the Sabbath, the Sabbath month contains the three feasts that foreshadow the time when we who are saved will go to the very dwelling place of God—heaven—and worship Him as we never have before!

The Feast of Trumpets foreshadows the event that marks the beginning of the Second Coming of Christ—the "rapture" of the Church. Humanity can be divided into two categories at the time of the rapture: those who are raptured—that is, caught up to be in the very presence of God—and those who are left behind. The Feast of Trumpets, Rosh Hashanah, foreshadows details concerning both destinies of humanity—the saved and the lost.

To understand the timing of the feasts, we must understand that the months of the Hebrew calendar revolve around the moon. Each month begins when there is just a thin crescent visible, signaling the new moon. Howard and Rosenthal point out for us:

> In relationship to the New Moon, Rosh Hashanah is unique. It is the only Jewish holiday which occurs on the first day of the month, at the New Moon, when the moon is dark and only a thin crescent. All other Jewish holidays occur later in their respective months when the moon is bright.[3]

The Feast of Trumpets occurs when the moon is at its darkest, foreshadowing the coming time when some of humanity will be left behind to suffer in the dark day of God's wrath. Howard and Rosenthal further tell us:

> Israel's prophets repeatedly warned of a coming dark day of judgment. They knew it as "the Day of the Lord," that terrible period of time at the end of this age when the Lord will pour out His fiery judgment.
>
> The prophet Amos spoke of this dark Day of Judgment: "Woe to you who desire the day of the Lord! For what good is the day of the Lord to you? It will be darkness, and not light. It will be as though a man fled from a lion, and a bear met him! Or as though he went into a house, leaned his hand on a wall, and a serpent bit him! Is not the day of the Lord darkness, and not light? Is it not very dark, with no brightness in it?" (Amos 5:18-20).
>
> The Hebrew prophet Zephaniah penned the ominous warning: "The great day of the Lord is near.... That day is a day of wrath, a day of trouble and distress, a day of devastation and desolation, a day of

darkness and gloominess, a day of clouds and thick darkness, a day of trumpet…" (Zephaniah 1:14-16).[4]

Those who are left behind will suffer in the dark days of the "tribulation," also known prophetically as Daniel's "seventieth week" (Daniel 9:20-27). The rest of humanity will be raptured into the presence of God. Paul writes,

> Listen, I tell you a mystery: We will not all sleep, but we will all be changed—in a flash, in the twinkling of an eye, at the last trumpet. For the trumpet will sound, the dead will be raised imperishable, and we will be changed (1 Corinthians 15:51-52).

The Feast of Trumpets, therefore, foreshadows for us the change that will take place in the "twinkling of an eye." The rapture of the Church, which Paul speaks of, will occur at the sound of the "last trumpet."

There is much division concerning the meaning of the last trumpet. Some believe that since it is the last trumpet, there must be a series of trumpets. In the Book of Revelation a series of trumpets is found in the middle of the tribulation; therefore, some reason that the Church must experience half of the tribulation before it is raptured. This has been labeled the "mid-tribulation theory."

John Hagee believes, however, that understanding the mores of that time period provides a better explanation. He believes that the last trumpet relates to the Hebrew betrothal custom. He explains:

> In a traditional ancient ceremony, the hopeful bridegroom went to the home of his potential bride carrying three things: his best financial offering, a betrothal contract, and a skin of wine. If the father was impressed and accepted the bridegroom's offering, he called the daughter for her response. If things were acceptable to her, the bride-to-be drank the wine, and immediately a trumpet sounded to announce their betrothal.
>
> During the following year of betrothal, the couple could not see each other alone, and a chaperone always

accompanied them wherever they went. During this year, the bridegroom went to his father's house to prepare a place, a *chupah*, or honeymoon bed.

When the young bridegroom was asked for the date of his wedding, he could only reply, "No man knows except my father." Why? Because he could not go get his bride until the father approved of his son's preparation.

The bride, therefore, had to be in a state of constant readiness lest the bridegroom's arrival catch her by surprise.

When the groom's father decided everything was in place and released his son to go fetch his bride, a second trumpet was blown. This trumpet, to announce the groom's coming, was called the "last trump."

Thus announced, the bridegroom took the marriage contract to present to the father of his intended bride. He claimed her as his bride and took her from her father's house to his father's house…That act was called the presentation.

After the presentation, the bridegroom would bring his bride to the place he had gone to prepare. There he would introduce her to all society of his friends who had heard the trumpet and come to celebrate the marriage feast.[5]

So we see that the "last trump" may refer to the time when our heavenly Bridegroom, Jesus Christ, returns to take us to the place He has prepared for us. Jesus assured us:

Do not let your hearts be troubled. Trust in God, trust also in me. In my Father's house are many rooms; if it were not so, I would have told you. I am going there to prepare a place for you. And if I go and prepare a place for you, I will come back and take you to be with me that you also may be where I am. (John 14:1-3)

The "last trump" represents the Second Coming of Christ; it was referred to as the "midnight cry" in Jesus' parable of the ten virgins (Matthew 25:6) and represents the rapture of the Church.

Since the fall of man, humanity has been in physical exile from the presence of God. The rapture represents the time of man's restoration to dwell in the presence of God in a new resurrection body. The apostle Paul writes:

> For the Lord himself will come down from heaven, with a loud command, with the voice of the archangel and with the trumpet call of God, and the dead in Christ will rise first. After that, we who are still alive and are left will be caught up together with them in the clouds to meet the Lord in the air. And we *will be with* the Lord forever." (1 Thessalonians 4:16-17, emphasis added)

There is an event that occurred on the day of the Feast of Trumpets, in which we see a foreshadowing of our restoration to dwell in the presence of God. God's Old Testament dwelling place among His people was the temple located in Jerusalem. Because of their disobedience, God allowed the Israelites to be conquered and driven out of the land of Judah. They lived as exiles in the land of the Babylonians under King Nebuchadnezzar.

When the Babylonians conquered Judah, they completely destroyed the temple. Later, when King Cyrus allowed the Israelites to return to the Promised Land, the first thing they did was to rebuild the altar of God. Joshua, the high priest, oversaw the building of the altar. We find recorded in Ezra 3:6: "On the first day of the seventh month [Feast of Trumpets] they began to offer burnt offerings to the Lord."

The analogy involves humanity's eventual restoration to dwell in God's presence. The Israelite's returned from exile to once again dwell in the Promised Land. They returned under the leadership of Joshua, the high priest, and were able to worship again at the altar of God—on the very day of the Feast of Trumpets! The name Joshua is the Hebrew equivalent of the Greek name Jesus. Jesus is our Great

High Priest. When we have been restored to dwell in the presence of God, we too will be able to worship at the altar of God under the leadership of our Great High Priest Jesus—beginning on the day of the Rapture.

The Day of Atonement
(Yom Kippur)

The second of the Fall Feasts is the Day of Atonement:

> The tenth day of this seventh month is the Day of Atonement. Hold a sacred assembly and deny yourselves, and present an offering made to the Lord by fire. Do no work on that day, because it is the Day of Atonement, when atonement is made for you before the Lord your God. (Leviticus 23:27-28)

The Day of Atonement was the holiest day of the calendar year. It was the only day of the year when someone was allowed to enter into the temple area known as the "Holy of Holies," where God's Shekinah glory once dwelt. The only one allowed entrance into the presence of God on this day was the high priest. Even then, he could only enter after undergoing a strict cleansing and purification ritual and making the appropriate sacrificial offering for his own sin.

The Glasers tell us: "It should especially be noted that the high priest was not required to wear the Urim and Thummim on the Day of Atonement. There was no need for those vestments, which were God's instruments of direct communication to the people, for on this day the high priest met God face to face."[6]

This was the day when the high priest would intervene on behalf of the people and make atonement for their sins of the past year. Howard and Rosenthal explain:

The High Priest

"Kippur is from the Hebrew word kaphar meaning, "to cover." Therefore, the word atonement simply means a covering." In making atonement for the people's sins, the high priest sought to "cover" their sins in an effort to hide them from God.

The atonement covering was the blood of the sacrificial animal. God instructed, "For the life of a creature is in the blood, and I have given it to you to make atonement for yourselves on the altar; it is the blood that makes atonement for one's life" (Leviticus 17:11).

In addition to the numerous sacrificial offerings that were made on this day, the center of attention was the offering of the two goats. As already discussed in our chapter "The Lamb of God," one of these two goats was the sacrificial goat; the other was the scapegoat. The goat to which the lot fell "for YHWH" (the original Hebrew name for God) was sacrificed and its blood was sprinkled by the high priest on the "mercy seat" for the atonement of the people's sins. The other goat (scapegoat) had the sins of the people confessed upon its forehead; it was then led far away into the wilderness—symbolically removing the people's sins forever.

Today the Israelites have a big problem concerning the Day of Atonement—and it is not a new problem. Since the day the temple was destroyed in A.D. 70, they have had no temple in which to worship. As a result, for nearly 2,000 years the Israelites have been unable to adequately participate in the Day of Atonement—the one day of the year when they could receive atonement for their sins! Therefore, they eagerly long for the day when their temple can be rebuilt and their worship of God can be restored so they can once again receive atonement for their sins!

But as we have discussed previously, they have an obstacle: the temple mount is not under their control because an Islamic shrine, called the Dome of the Rock, now rests there! Hence, they can only dream of the day when the temple can be rebuilt.

What they don't understand is that the temple of God has already been rebuilt! As discussed earlier, one of the first accomplishments of Joshua the high priest, after the return of God's people from their exile in Babylon, was the restoration of the altar of God. This was the first act completed in an effort to rebuild the temple and restore the worship of God.

This foreshadowed what our Great High Priest Jesus (Greek for Joshua), accomplished through His finished work at Calvary and His sending of the Counselor or Holy Spirit. Because of the indwelling of God's Holy Spirit, our body becomes God's temple where He can be worshiped in spirit and in truth. Paul explains, "Don't you know that you yourselves are God's temple and that God's Spirit lives in you?" (1 Corinthians 3:16). *The Temple has been restored and it is the living temple—the church!*

Jesus is the fulfillment of every aspect of the Day of Atonement. Concerning the offering of the sacrifice, the Glasers point out:

> What purpose then did the Old Testament sacrifices serve? After all, they were given to Israel by God Himself (Leviticus 1-7). The animal sacrifices taught the Israelites that the gruesome penalty for sin was death. They demonstrated that God was gracious in allowing substitutes to pay that terrible penalty. But the sacrificial system was a type, a foreshadowing, of God's ultimate sacrifice for sin, Jesus the Messiah.[8]

Jesus is the fulfillment of the high priest as well. He is the only one worthy to enter into the presence of God to make atonement for our sins. We're told:

> Therefore, brothers, since we have confidence to enter the Most Holy Place by the blood of Jesus, by a new and living way opened for us through the curtain, that is, his body, and since we have a *great priest* over the house of God, let us draw near to God with a sincere heart in full assurance of faith, having our hearts sprinkled to cleanse us from a guilty conscience and having our bodies washed with pure water (Hebrews 10:19-22, emphasis added).

As our High Priest, Jesus has restored God's temple by creating the living temple—the Church. He has repaired the altar of sacrifice by His finished work on the cross. He is the meaning behind the sacrificial goat—we are cleansed by the blood of Lamb. He is also the fulfillment of the scapegoat. Consequently, "As far as the east is from the west, so far has he removed our transgressions from us" (Psalm 103:12).

Further, the Day of Atonement foreshadows the next event after the fulfillment of the Feast of Trumpets. After the Rapture of the Church occurs, there will be a time of judgment.

Those left behind will suffer through God's judgment on this world, also known as the time of "tribulation." This time is also referred to in the Scriptures as Daniel's seventieth week and the time of "Jacob's trouble." Ultimately, those left behind all will stand before the Great White Throne, and be "judged according to what they had done as recorded in the books" (Revelation 20:12).

Those who have received Christ as their Savior also will stand in judgment—before the judgment seat of Christ. "For we must all appear before the judgment seat of Christ, that each one may receive what is due him for the things done while in the body, whether good or bad" (2 Corinthians 5:10). This judgment occurs in heaven, after those who are marked with the seal of the Holy Spirit have been raptured.

A passage of Scripture concerning the Day of Atonement, taken from God's instructions to Moses as recorded in Leviticus 23, gives us insight into the judgment of those who are in Christ. "The tenth day of this seventh month is the Day of Atonement. Hold a sacred assembly and deny yourselves, and *present an offering made to the Lord by fire*" (verse 27, emphasis added). On the Day of Atonement, those who have been redeemed (saved) will present themselves as an offering *"made to the Lord by fire."*

The apostle Paul further tells us concerning the judgment of the redeemed, "His work will be shown for what it is, because the Day will bring it to light. It will be *revealed with fire*, and the fire will test the quality of each man's work. If what he has built survives, he will receive his reward. If it is burned up, he will suffer loss; he himself will be saved, but only as one escaping through the flames" (1 Corinthians 3:13-15, emphasis added). So, the judgment of those in Christ will be a refining by fire. Everything that does not bring glory to Christ will be burned up, while those acts that are glorifying to Christ will survive the refining fire and bring heavenly rewards.

Furthermore, we are told that one of the rewards will be the fine linen that we, as the bride of Christ, will wear to the wedding supper of the Lamb. "Let us rejoice and be glad and give him glory! For the wedding of the Lamb has come, and his bride has made herself ready. Fine linen, bright and clean, was given her to wear. *(Fine linen stands for the righteous acts of the saints)*" (Revelation 19:7-8, emphasis added).

Paul stated that if our works are consumed by fire, we will suffer loss but we will be saved "as one escaping through the flames." It is significant that this judgment is for those whose names are written in the Lamb's book of life—believers in the Lord Jesus Christ! No one who stands before the judgment seat of Christ will perish! Even though our works may be burned up, we ourselves will be saved!

Leviticus 23:28 gives us insight into this truth as well. "*Do no work* on that day, because it is the Day of Atonement, when atonement is made for you before the Lord your God" (emphasis added). So, there is no work we *can do* that will save us and allow our names to be written in the Lamb's book of life! Paul explains, "For it is by grace you have been saved, through faith—and this not from yourselves, it is the gift of God—*not by works*, so that no one can boast" (Ephesians 2:8-9, emphasis added). Only the atoning blood of the Lamb of God can save us. If everything else is burned up, we will receive atonement and escape the flames because of God's gracious gift of the blood of the Lamb.

Feast of Tabernacles
(Sukkot)

The Feast of Tabernacles is the seventh and final Feast of the Lord:

> On the fifteenth day of the seventh month the Lord's Feast of Tabernacles begins, and it lasts for seven days. (Leviticus 23:34)

It is no coincidence that the last of the Feasts of the Lord was the seventh feast. Seven is the symbolic number of *completion.* When God created the world, we are told that on the seventh day He rested. "By the seventh day God had finished the work he had been doing; so on the seventh day he rested from all his work. And God blessed the seventh day and made it holy, because on it he rested from all the work of creating that he had done" (Genesis 2:2-3). Why did God rest on the seventh day? It wasn't because He was tired! He was revealing to us prophetic details concerning what He would do in the future. Just as there are seven days in the week, there are seven Feasts of the Lord.

The Glasers point out, concerning the sacrificial offerings made during the Feast of Tabernacles:

> A fascinating and mysterious pattern emerges from the seemingly endless list of sacrifices. No matter how the offerings are grouped or counted, their number always remains divisible by the number seven. During the week are offered 70 bullocks, 14 rams, and 98 lambs—altogether 182 sacrifices (26 x 7), to which must be added 336 (48 x 7) tenths of ephahs of flour for the meal offering.
>
> It was no coincidence that this seven-day holiday, which took place in the height of the seventh month, had the perfect number, seven, imprinted on its sacrifices.[9]

The seventh feast is symbolic of the completion of God's work. So, this seventh feast foreshadows the time when the new covenant time period will come to completion and the Lord will establish His millennial kingdom here on earth.

Rosenthal and Howard tell us: "The Feast of Tabernacles is known by at least two names in Scripture. Most often it is referred to as *Sukkot,* or "Tabernacles." The English word "tabernacle" is from the Latin *tabernaculum* meaning "booth" or "hut."[10] During this seven-day feast, the Israelites commemorated the time when they dwelt in the wilderness after their exodus from Egypt. During their sojourn in the wilderness, they lived in temporary dwellings or booths, and God provided for their every need. Likewise, the Israelites would construct booths out of palm leaves, olive branches, and other materials, and live in them during the seven days of this feast.

The other scriptural term for this feast was "The Feast of Ingathering." It was so called because it occurred at the end of the fall harvest, when the harvest was complete and being gathered in. The two scriptural names for the feast foreshadow for us the time when God's harvest of souls will be complete and God will provide for our every need in ways He never has before.

The Temple Dedication

It was on the day of the Feast of Tabernacles that Solomon dedicated the temple of the Lord. Solomon's father, David, had the plans for the temple—and his son carried them out. "When all the work Solomon had done for the temple of the Lord was finished, he brought in the things his father David had dedicated—the silver and gold and all the furnishings—and he placed them in the treasuries of God's temple" (2 Chronicles 5:1).

After the dedication of the temple, we are told "the glory of the Lord filled the temple of God" (2 Chronicles 7:1). But God's people would soon turn from Him and serve idols. So God allowed the temple and their nation to be destroyed; and they were taken into exile, separated from the place where God's presence once dwelt.

After the seventy years of exile in Babylon, the Israelites were allowed to return to Jerusalem. One of the first things that they did was rebuild the altar of God, which was overseen by the high priest Joshua. We are told in Nehemiah 8:1, 14, and 17:

> When the seventh month came and the Israelites had
> settled in their towns, all the people assembled as one
> man in the square before the Water Gate. They told
> Ezra the scribe to bring out the Book of the Law of
> Moses, which the Lord had commanded for Israel...
> They found written in the Law, which the Lord had
> commanded through Moses, that the Israelites were

to live in booths during the feast of the seventh month... The whole company that had returned from exile built booths and lived in them. From the days of Joshua son of Nun until that day, the Israelites had not celebrated it like this. And their joy was very great.

Likewise, we find the *fulfillment* of these two historical prophecies in that God the Father had the plans for His temple; His Son Jesus completed them. The temple is not a man-made structure—but a *living temple* called the Church. Just as Solomon brought the silver and gold that had been dedicated by his father into the temple, Jesus will bring into His temple treasury those who have been dedicated to His Father. Just as the Israelites celebrated the Feast of Tabernacles after their return from exile, the Feast of Tabernacles foreshadows for us the day when we who have been in exile from dwelling in the presence of God will be allowed to return to the throne room of God and worship in His presence once more. It will be a day of perfect peace and perfect rest when God will restore us to fellowship with Him and provide for every need.

The Sabbath—Rest

Just as the seventh day of the week was a day of rest, the seventh feast was a feast of rest. The fourth of the Ten Commandments states: "Observe the Sabbath day by keeping it holy, as the Lord your God has commanded you. Six days you shall labor and do all your work, but the seventh day is a Sabbath to the Lord your God. On it you shall not do any work" (Deuteronomy 5:12-14). So we are not surprised to find that the Sabbath-rest feast is likewise a feast of rest.

It is interesting to note that not only were God's people to have a day of rest but the land was to have a sabbath year of rest as well. "When you enter the land I am going to give you, the land itself must observe a sabbath to the Lord. For six years sow your fields, and for six years prune your vineyards and gather their crops. But in the seventh year the land is to have a sabbath of rest, a sabbath to the Lord" (Leviticus 25:2-4). Jeffrey gives the following insight.

There is no scriptural evidence that Israel ever faithfully kept the law of the Sabbath of the land by letting the land fallow for a whole year. Once Israel adopted a monarchy under King Saul in 1096 B.C., for the first time, the law of the Sabbath of the land could have been enforced by royal decree. However, Israel did not obey God in this matter, and 490 years later, in 606 B.C., she had missed keeping this Sabbath a total of seventy times. Moses prophesied more than 850 years earlier that Israel would disobey this Sabbath law and would go into captivity for her disobedience. "Then shall the land enjoy her Sabbaths, as long as it lieth desolate, and ye be in your enemies land; even then shall the land rest;...because it did not rest in your Sabbaths, when ye dwelt upon it." (Leviticus 26:34-35)[11]

The Scriptures record in Jeremiah 25:11 Jeremiah's prophecy that Israel would be in captivity in Babylon for seventy years. Second Chronicles 36:21 further explains that the seventy years of exile were punishment for disobeying the law of the Sabbath-rest of the land. "The land enjoyed its sabbath rests; all the time of its desolation it rested, until the seventy years were completed in fulfillment of the word of the Lord spoken by Jeremiah." In other words, the Lord forced Israel to obey the Sabbath-rest of the land! If they would not obey the Sabbath-rest voluntarily—then they would suffer the punishment of the Lord.

The Feast of Tabernacles is the "Sabbath-rest" feast and is symbolic of the millennial reign of Christ (the physical thousand-year reign of Christ on the earth) that will be a time of *perfect rest*. The prophet Isaiah describes it as a day when, "The wolf will live with the lamb, the leopard will lie down with the goat, the calf and the lion and the yearling together; and a little child will lead them" (Isaiah 11:6).

The Ceremonies

There were two ceremonies associated with the Feast of Tabernacles: the Water-Libation ceremony and the Temple-Lighting ceremony. Each morning of the feast, the high priest would draw water from the Pool of Siloam and enter the temple area through the Water Gate. "As he entered, three blasts of the silver trumpets sounded from the temple, and the priests with one voice repeated the words of Isaiah, 'Therefore with joy you will draw water from the wells of salvation' (Isaiah 12:3)."[12]

Every evening, beginning with the second evening, four enormous menorahs were lit and illuminated the temple mount. "The light celebration was reminiscent of the descent of the Shekinah glory in Solomon's day and looked forward to the return of the Shekinah in the days of the Messiah."[13]

In the seventh and eighth chapters of John's gospel, we are told of a journey that Jesus made to Jerusalem at the time of the Feast of Tabernacles. During the feast, He explained that He was the fulfillment of the two ceremonies. "On the last and greatest day of the Feast, Jesus stood and said in a loud voice, 'If anyone is thirsty, let him come to me and drink. Whoever believes in me, as the Scripture has said, streams of living water will flow from within him'" (John 7:37-38). And, "When Jesus spoke again to the people, he said, 'I am the light of the world. Whoever follows me will never walk in darkness, but will have the light of life'" (John 8:12).

Fulfillment of the Fall Feasts

The apostle Paul understood the true meaning of the Feasts of the Lord as he explained, "These are a shadow of the things that were to come; the reality, however, is found in Christ" (Colossians 2:17). The Spring Feasts foreshadow the first Advent of Christ as He fulfilled His role as the suffering Savior. The Fall Feasts foreshadow the events of Christ's Second Coming when He will fulfill His role as the King of Kings and Lord of Lords. The Feast of Trumpets foreshadows the rapture of the church when those who have received Christ as their Savior will be taken to be in the presence of God and those who have rejected Christ will be left behind to suffer God's wrath. The Day of Atonement foreshadows the time of God's judgment on this world and the atonement that those who are saved will receive at the judgment seat of Christ. The seven-day Feast of Tabernacles foreshadows the millennial kingdom, which Christ will establish; it will be a time of complete peace when God will wipe away every tear! (See Figures 3 and 4 on page 102)

We are therefore living in the "summertime," the time between Christ's fulfillment of the Spring Feasts and His eventual fulfillment of the Fall Feasts. But we need not live in fear if we have been spiritually immunized. Just as the "killed" polio vaccine brought peace of mind to those who were immunized in the 1950s, we who have received the spiritual vaccination of God's Holy Spirit can live in the peace of mind regarding the events that will occur at the Second Coming of Christ. We can look forward to the return of Christ— just as the Israelites looked forward to the winter rains that brought about the fall harvest.

Figures 3 & 4

Figure 3

CHRIST'S FULFILLMENT OF THE FALL FEASTS

FALL FEAST	**FULFILLMENT**
Trumpets (Rosh Hashanah)	Rapture of Church
Day of Atonement (Yom Kippur)	Judgment
Tabernacles (Sukkot)	Millennial Reign

Figure 4

CHRIST'S FULFILLMENT
OF THE FEASTS OF THE LORD

SPRING	**FALL**
Redemption	Rapture – Judgment – Millennial Reign
Forgiveness	
Eternal Life	
Holy Spirit	

— CHAPTER FIVE QUESTIONS —

1. The three fall feasts occur during the seventh month.
   a. What is the significance of the number seven?
   b. Where else in the Scriptures does the number seven play a symbolic role?

2. The author points out that the Feast of Trumpets foreshadows the rapture of the Church as well as the "dark day of God's wrath" upon those who are left behind. Review Jesus' Parables of the Ten Virgins (Matthew 25:1-13) and the Sheep and the Goats (Matthew 25:31-46).
   a. What does the "midnight cry" represent?
   b. What is the destiny of the five wise virgins and the sheep?
   c. What is the final destiny of the five foolish virgins and the goats?
   d. What could the oil in the lamps represent?

3. In what ways will Jesus fulfill the Day of Atonement? Consider the meaning of:
   a. Atonement
   b. High Priest
   c. Sacrifice
   d. Scapegoat

4. Concerning the observance of the Day of Atonement, God commanded: "present an offering made to the Lord by fire" (Leviticus 23:27). Based upon Paul's words contained in 1 Corinthians 3:13-15, the author states: "those who have been redeemed (saved) will present themselves as an offering "made to the Lord by fire." Review Daniel 3:7-30. How could this passage be a foreshadowing of the future Day of Atonement?

5. As a foreshadowing of the millennial reign of Christ, what is the significance of the following aspects of the Feast of Tabernacles?
   a.   Temporary dwellings
   b.   Sabbath-rest
   c.   Ingathering
   d.   Water libation ceremony
   e.   Temple-Lighting ceremony

6. Jesus has already fulfilled the meaning of the Spring Feasts and He fulfilled them on the very day of each feast. Realizing that truth, can we predict which day of the calendar year the rapture of the Church might occur?

IMMANUEL

Therefore the Lord himself will give you a sign:
The virgin will be with child and will give birth to
a son, and will call him Immanuel. — Isaiah 7:14

I heard his story soon after I arrived at work one morning. His name was Russell Patterson. He was in his mid-thirties and taught Sunday school at a local church. Although we weren't formally introduced, I learned a great deal about his life and circumstances from one of my partners who attended church with him. A few days earlier, he was skiing with his family in the Rockies, when his speech became slurred. The results of his diagnostic tests showed that he had a mass in his brain that, by radiologic scans, appeared to be a high-grade malignant tumor.

I watched from across the room as his head was shaved and he was prepped for the operating room. A little while later, I happened to be standing at the operating suite door, the only way into the operating rooms. I was having a conversation with someone as Russell was being wheeled past me. Our eyes met for a brief instant, and in that moment he said something to me. Now I probably couldn't tell you what I ate for lunch yesterday. And I certainly don't remember to whom I was talking or what we were talking about as Russell passed by; but I will always remember those three words Russell said to me. "Bless you, Brother."

I suppose it impacted me so profoundly because I knew Russell was in the midst of a terrible storm in his life. The fear of the unknown had to be crashing down on him. Will the tumor be malignant? Will they be able to remove it completely? Will I survive the operation? Will I feel any pain? Those questions and fears, as well as many more, had to be going through his mind as he was transported toward the operating room; yet as he passed by, he paused to bless me—a perfect stranger. And I was indeed blessed! For a brief moment, the paths of our lives crossed and my life was forever changed! I will always remember how Russell Patterson paused during one of the greatest storms of his life to bless me.

I saw Russell again a few months later on the Discovery Channel. Russell was one of their main stories during a special report on Duke Hospital. He was taking part in an experimental procedure to eradicate his cancer. Part of the treatment involved brain surgery while Russell remained awake under local anesthesia. Russell's tumor was very close to his speech center; therefore, surgeons had Russell talk with them during the surgery so they could monitor his speech.

This type of procedure is possible because God, in His great wisdom, created the brain to contain a miniature blueprint of the body. "Homunculus," is the term given for the topographical manifestation of the body on the cerebral cortex of the brain. Stimulate a part of the homunculus, and it will be manifested in the corresponding part of the body. How wonderful it is that God gave us a blueprint to aid in our treatment and understanding of our current dwelling place—the human body.

Immanuel

In a similar manner, God has also given us a blueprint of His dwelling place among humanity. The blueprint involves an understanding of the term Immanuel – *God with us*! Isaiah 7:14 tells us of an incredible irony: God, the creator of the universe, allowed Himself to be created! The Omnipotent would become an infant, wear diapers, and wean from his mother's breast! And through His incarnation would come a great sign—the virgin birth.

It's only one word — *Immanuel.* But wrapped up in that one word is the entirety of the Scriptures. In the beginning God dwelt in the very presence of man. But because of man's sin, there came a separation. God cast man out of the Garden of Eden, so he could no longer partake of the tree of life and spend an eternity separated from God. However, God's plan was, once again, for the dwelling of God to be among His creation. God's plan and His love for man were greater than man's failure! His plan for reestablishing His dwelling place among humankind was fulfilled by the meaning of that one word—*Immanuel.*

Immanuel finds its origin in God's final words to Satan as Adam and Eve were about to be driven out of the garden: "And I will put enmity between you and the woman, and between your offspring and hers; he will crush your head, and you will strike his heel" (Genesis 3:15). This "he" God mentions—whom Satan will injure, but who will ultimately destroy Satan—is Christ.

But notice also that "he" is referred to as the "offspring" of woman. Here in the third chapter of Genesis, we are given a prophecy that Christ would be born of a woman. Isaiah 7:14 adds more information: it would be a virgin birth and the male child would be called Immanuel.

There are those who doubt the reality of the virgin birth. As I discussed in chapter two, "The Lamb of God," it is my opinion that God caused Sarah to wait until she was at age ninety (well past menopause) so that there could be no doubt that Isaac's birth, foreshadowing the birth of Christ, involved a divine intervention of God.

The Tabernacle — God's Temporary Dwelling Place

Nowhere are we given more prophetic details concerning God's dwelling place among mankind, Immanuel, than in the Scriptures concerning the tabernacle. As Moses received the word of God on Mount Horeb, he also received the details of God's temporary dwelling place among His people—the tabernacle. As God's dwelling place among humanity, the tabernacle therefore, foreshadows for us Immanuel—literally God dwelling among man!

In his Gospel, John introduces Immanuel to us by saying, "In the beginning was the Word, and the Word was with God, and the Word was God...The Word became flesh and *made his dwelling among us*" (John 1:1,14, emphasis added). The Greek word for "dwelling" is *skênoô*, which literally means "tabernacled." The literal translation of John 1:14 is: "The Word became flesh and tabernacled among us." Therefore, in giving Moses the details for the tabernacle, in reality God was giving us details about the One who would tabernacle among us—Christ!

Furthermore, in 1 Corinthians 12:27, the apostle Paul tells us that the Church is the "body of Christ." The first physical church structure was the tabernacle. As we said earlier, just as the homunculus is a blueprint of the body as a whole, the tabernacle serves as God's divine blueprint of Christ. Therefore, as we survey the many details of the tabernacle (God's dwelling place), we are in fact learning details about Immanuel.

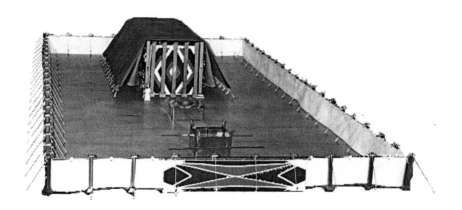

The Tabernacle

Let's take an imaginary tour of the tabernacle. The first noteworthy feature is that almost all of the objects making up the tabernacle are made of wood that is overlaid with gold. Here we see a foreshadowing of the incarnation of Immanuel. The wood symbolizes His mortality and the gold symbolizes His divine nature. Just as the structures of the tabernacle contained both wood and gold, Jesus was both God and man in one person.

Approaching the tabernacle as it stood in the wilderness, the white outer curtain first catches our attention. White stands in stark contrast to the myriad browns that dominate the desert landscape. Throughout the Scriptures the color white is used to symbolize purity or holiness. Therefore, the outer curtain speaks of Christ's sanctification. He was in the world but not of the world.

As we arrive at the outer curtain, we find there is *only one* gateway through which we can access the tabernacle. Likewise, there is *only one way* for us to enter into the presence of God—through Jesus Christ! Jesus said, "*I am the gate,* whoever enters through me will be saved." And further, "*I am the way* and the truth and the life. No one comes to the Father *except through me*" (John 10:9; 14:6, emphasis added).

Sacrificial Altar

Once through the door, the first structure that we encounter is the sacrificial altar. It is here that we see Christ foreshadowed as the "Lamb of God who takes away the sin of the world" (John 1:29). The altar of sacrifice represents what Christ did for us on the cross. He became the ram with his head caught in the thorns, which Jehovah-jireh provided for the sacrifice in place of Isaac. Unlike the Israelites who worshiped in the tabernacle, we may continue past the sacrificial altar towards the very presence of God because "Christ, our Passover lamb, has been sacrificed" (1 Corinthians 5:7).

Laver

Next, as we journey toward God's dwelling place, we arrive at the laver—a basin of water provided for the priests' purification. As the priests stopped to cleanse themselves with the water from the laver, they probably remembered the words spoken by Moses: "Whenever they enter the [tabernacle], they shall wash with water so that they will not die" (Exodus 30:20). This washing made the priests ceremonially clean so that they could worship in the presence of God's dwelling place. When studying Jesus' first miracle (turning water into wine), we learned that the key to understanding that miracle was the type of jars He used. They were "the kind used by the Jews for ceremonial washing" (John 2:6). The water that cleansed the priests outwardly was turned into wine that symbolized the blood of Jesus, which cleanses us inwardly.

At the Last Supper, Jesus said the wine represented His blood that was shed for our sins. The laver, therefore, foreshadows that it is the blood of Christ that cleanses us before God and allows us to worship Him. This truth is further explained in Hebrews 9:14: "How much more, then, will the blood of Christ, who through the eternal Spirit offered himself unblemished to God, cleanse our consciences from

The Holy Place and the Holy of Holies

acts that lead to death, so that we may serve the living God!" Now cleansed, we may enter the tabernacle itself. The tabernacle is divided into two areas: The Holy Place and the Holy of Holies, which are separated by a veil.

Table of Unleavened Bread

As we enter the Holy Place, we notice three pieces of furniture. To our right, is the "table of the bread of the presence." On this table would be twelve loaves of unleavened bread. Jesus said, "*I am the bread of life.* He who comes to me will never go hungry" (John 6:35, emphasis added). As mentioned earlier, leaven (yeast) is symbolic of sin. So we see that Jesus is the *fulfillment* of the unleavened bread—He was without sin!

Lampstand

Turning to our left, we see the lampstand that supplies the light that allows us to worship in the darkness of the tabernacle. Isaiah prophesied, "The people walking in darkness have seen a great light; on those living in the land of the shadow of death a light has dawned...For to us a child is born" (Isaiah 9:2,6). Jesus, the fulfillment of the promised child, proclaimed, "*I am the light* of the world. Whoever follows me will never walk in darkness, but will have the light of life" (John 8:12, emphasis added). Jesus was the fulfillment of the lampstand—He was the "great light" and the "light of the world" that allows us to worship God and "not walk in darkness."

Altar of Incense

The third item of furniture in the Holy Place was the altar of incense. It is located straight ahead of us against the veil that separates the Holy Place from the Holy of Holies. Priests used this altar to offer up prayers on behalf of the people. The incense symbolically carries their prayers upward toward God. It is here that we learn that just as the high priests were the mediators between God and man, Jesus is now our great High Priest—the mediator between God and humankind. Therefore, we are to pray in the name of Jesus.

The veil that separates the Holy of Holies from the rest of the tabernacle also served to separate man from the very presence of God. Only the high priest could enter through the veil; and that was permitted only one day each year—on the Day of Atonement. Christ has permanently removed the veil of man's separation from God's presence by His finished work on the cross! The Gospel of Matthew tells us that at the moment Christ died on the cross, "The curtain of the temple was torn in two from top to bottom" (Matthew 27:51).

Veil

The curtain (veil) represents the body of Christ that was broken so we could have access to the presence of God. The Scriptures further tell us: "Therefore, brothers, since we have confidence to enter the Most Holy Place by the blood of Jesus, by a new and living way opened for us through the [veil], that is, his body, and since we have a great priest over the house of God, let us draw near to God with a sincere heart in full assurance of faith" (Hebrews 10:19-22, emphasis added).

Once inside the Most Holy Place, we see only one piece of furniture—the Ark of the Covenant. The top covering of the ark is known as the mercy seat. It was here that God was enthroned between the cherubim. Inside the ark were only three objects: the tablets of the law, the pot of

Ark of the Covenant

manna, and Aaron's rod. In each of these, we see information about Christ.

The tablets of the law (Ten Commandments) were the very Word of God. Referring to Jesus, John tells us "the Word was God" and "The Word became flesh and made his dwelling among us" (John 1:2,14).

Manna was called the "bread from heaven." On one occasion the Pharisees came to Jesus and demanded a sign:

> So they asked him, "What miraculous sign then will you give that we may see it and believe you? What will you do? Our forefathers ate the manna in the desert; as it is written: 'He gave them bread from heaven to eat.'"

> Jesus said to them, "I tell you the truth, it is not Moses who has given you the bread from heaven, but it is my Father who gives you the true bread from heaven. For *the bread of God is he who comes down from heaven and gives life to the world.*" (John 6:30-33, emphasis added)

And lastly, Aaron's rod was a sign of the chosen one. The Israelites in the wilderness were questioning the leadership of Moses and Aaron (the high priest). So Moses had each tribe bring a rod with the tribe's name written on it. The tribe of Levi was written on Aaron's rod. Of the twelve rods, whichever produced buds by the next morning would be God's choice as His high priest. When morning came, Aaron's rod had not only budded, but also produced the fruit of almonds! Here we see Christ, not only as the chosen one and Great High Priest, but also prophecy concerning His death and resurrection. The dead rod came to life and produced fruit. Christ died, rose from the dead, and shared with us the fruit of the Holy Spirit!

Truly in the topography of the tabernacle (as it is described in God's Word) we see a divine blueprint of Christ—the Word that became flesh and temporarily tabernacled among us. The wood overlaid with gold speaks of His union as man and God. The outer curtain speaks of His sanctification. He is the door that leads to the presence of God. He is the sacrifice for our sins, and it is by His blood that we are cleansed before God. He is the unleavened bread and the light of the world. He is our mediator through whom we pray. His body was broken to remove our separation from God. He is our Great High Priest. He is the Word that became flesh and the chosen one that was resurrected from the dead. *He was God's dwelling place among man—Immanuel.*

The Temple — God's Permanent Dwelling Place

The tabernacle was a temporary dwelling place for God. God designed it to be disassembled and transported from place to place. When the Shekinah glory of God would rise and move, the Levites would disassemble the tabernacle and transport it to the new place

God chose. The temporary tabernacle would later be replaced by a more permanent dwelling place for God—the temple.

David was given the plans for the temple; but he wasn't allowed to build it. Why not? Why did the temple have to be built by his son? All we are told is,

> David said to Solomon: "My son, I had it in my heart to build a house for the Name of the Lord my God. But this word of the Lord came to me: 'You have shed much blood and have fought many wars. You are not to build a house for my Name, because you have shed much blood on the earth in my sight.'" (1 Chronicles 22:7-8)

David was truly a man of warfare. Yet didn't God ordain those wars? Didn't God command the Israelites to drive out the inhabitants of the Promised Land? Didn't God give them great victories when they were obedient and followed His commands? Why should that prevent David from building the temple? I believe what we see here is the same pattern that prompted the writing of this book. We have a prophetic foreshadowing of what God would accomplish through His Son. The answer to our questions is found as we continue to read David's address to his son, Solomon:

> But you will have a son who will be a man of peace and rest, and I will give him rest from all his enemies on every side. His name will be Solomon, and I will grant Israel peace and quiet during his reign. He is the one who will build a house for my Name. He will be my son, and I will be his father. And I will establish the throne of his kingdom over Israel forever. (1 Chronicles 22:9-10)

At first glance, this passage seems to mean that God is speaking about Solomon. Especially since God says, *"His name will be Solomon."* Actually, God is not talking about David's son. We can know this for several reasons.

We need look no further than the last verse of that passage, "And I will establish the throne of his kingdom over Israel forever."

Solomon's throne over Israel did not last forever. If this is only taken literally to mean David's son, many pieces don't fit and questions remain unanswered. Therefore, we must look for a deeper, prophetic meaning.

The "son" God was speaking of was God's Son—Jesus Christ. God said to David, "He will be my son, and *I will be his father.*" Further, the name *Solomon* means "peace." Jesus is the "Son of David" (Matthew 12:23) and the "king of peace" (Hebrews 7:2). It is His kingdom that will last forever. Therefore, what God is revealing to us through this passage is that the temporary dwelling place of God among His people would be replaced by a more permanent dwelling place. Just as David had the plans for the temple that were carried out through his son, Solomon, God the Father's plans for His more permanent temple would be carried out by His Son—Jesus!

The temple that Solomon built was destroyed and rebuilt twice. The last temple, Herod's temple, was standing during the time of Jesus. As Jesus and His disciples were leaving it on one occasion, Jesus made a remarkable prediction: "One of his disciples said to him, 'Look, Teacher! What massive stones! What magnificent buildings!' 'Do you see all these great buildings?' replied Jesus. 'Not one stone here will be left on another; every one will be thrown down'" (Mark 13:1-2). About thirty years after Jesus made that prediction, it came to pass as the Romans completely destroyed the temple! And it has never been rebuilt! There presently stands upon the temple mount an Islamic shrine called the Dome of the Rock.

Even as I write these words, there is fighting going on between the Jews and the Muslims in Palestine. Both sides want control of the land of Palestine, and the most prized piece of property is the Temple Mount in Jerusalem.

There are three groups of people living in Jerusalem: the Jews, the Muslims, and the Christians. So why don't we hear about Christians joining in the fight for control of the Temple Mount? And what was God's purpose in not allowing the rebuilding of the temple? There is no need for the physical temple because the more permanent temple (the dwelling place of God among humanity) has already been rebuilt. It is the living temple built by God's Son, the Son of David, and the Prince of Peace—Jesus Christ Himself! The apostle Paul explains, "Don't you know that you yourselves are God's temple and that God's Spirit lives in you?" (1 Corinthians 3:16). The physical temple structure has never been rebuilt because it is no longer needed! It has been replaced by the living temple—God's people.

God with Us

The Tabernacle (God's temporary dwelling among humanity) *foreshadowed* for us the life of Jesus, who "tabernacled" among us in the flesh only *temporarily*. The temple (God's more permanent dwelling built by the Son according to the Father's plans) *foreshadowed* for us that God would restore His dwelling place among humankind *permanently*. "For we are the temple of the living God" (2 Corinthians 6:16). Because God has provided a way to dwell among us through His Holy Spirit, there is no longer a need for a physical temple.

The Book of Revelation gives us the end of the story concerning Immanuel: "I saw the Holy City, the new Jerusalem, coming down out of heaven from God…I did not see a temple in the city, because the Lord God Almighty and the Lamb are its temple" (Revelation 21:2,22).

The tabernacle, and later the more permanent temple, were divine blueprints that the Great Physician used to reveal to us information concerning another of God's dwelling places—Immanuel. Because of what Christ accomplished in fulfilling His role as Immanuel, we have become the replacement of the temple—God's more permanent dwelling place. As amazing as it seems, *God dwells within us through His Holy Spirit!* Just as Russell Patterson blessed me with three profound words, God has done likewise. He has blessed us with Immanuel—*God with us*. What a blessing indeed!

— CHAPTER SIX QUESTIONS —

1. The author states, "in giving Moses the details for the tabernacle, in reality God was giving us details about the One who would tabernacle among us—Christ!" Review how the many aspects of the tabernacle were prophecy concerning Christ:
   a. God's temporary
      dwelling among man
   b. Wood overlaid with gold
   c. The white outer curtain
   d. The solitary gate
   e. The sacrificial altar
   f. The laver of cleansing
   g. The unleavened bread
   h. The light
   i. The altar of incense
   j. The veil
   k. The Ark of the Covenant
   l. The Word of God
   m. The manna
   n. Aaron's rod that budded

2. Review Numbers 9:15-23.
   a. Could there be a reason for the redundancy in the passage?
   b. What does it teach us about how God wants us to follow Him today?

3. The temple, as God's permanent dwelling place among mankind, replaced the tabernacle.
   a. What did the temple foreshadow as God's current dwelling place among humankind?
   b. Realizing that the priests had to be ceremonial clean before worshiping in God's temple, what application can be made about our worship of God today?

4. God gave David the plans for the temple, but wouldn't allow him to build it.

a. Why do you believe David was not allowed to build the temple?

b. Could God have been revealing to us information about His Son's role in building the current temple?

c. When Jesus said He could rebuild the temple in three days, what truth was He conveying?

5. God's Word was contained in the Ark of the Covenant that was located in the Holy of Holies. What inference can be made of where God wants His Word to be located today?

6. Review 2 Samuel 6:1-7.

a. Why was Uzzah struck dead?

b. How was the Ark supposed to be transported? (See Numbers 4:15)

c. How does God want us to transport His Word today?

THE BRIDEGROOM

The bride belongs to the bridegroom.
—John 3:29

$\mathcal{D}$r. Crawford Long of Jefferson, Georgia is given the credit for first using diethyl ether vapor to produce surgical anesthesia in 1842. However, due to a lack of publicity, the method of using inhaled anesthesia was not embraced until Dr. William Morton demonstrated it in Boston in 1846. The following year, in January 1847, Dr. James Simpson used inhaled chloroform to produce anesthesia during the delivery of a baby in England. From an account of Dr. Simpson's life story, we're told the following:

> Simpson's report of his success with chloroform appeared almost within a week of the first case, but instead of leading to the rapid adoption of anesthesia in obstetrical practice, as the reports of Morton's success in Boston had caused the rapid adoption of anesthesia in surgery, it led to a stormy controversy. Simpson and the use of chloroform were denounced from the pulpit and in pamphlet. The main theme of the argument against him was that pain, especially the pain of childbirth, was the ordained lot of mankind. Preventing pain was sacrilege. Chloroform was denounced "as a decoy of Satan, apparently offering itself to bless women; but in the end it will harden society and rob God of the deep, earnest cries which arise in time of trouble for help." The

authority quoted by the ecclesiastical attacks was the biblical curse put on mankind in Genesis 3:16: "Unto the woman he said, I will greatly multiply thy sorrow and thy conception; in sorrow thou shall bring forth children...." Sorrow meant pain, they claimed, and prevention of pain during childbirth "was contrary to religion and the express command of the Scripture." Simpson replied with logic and Scripture of his own. He pointed to inconsistencies in the following of other scriptural admonitions, particularly in regard to agricultural practices, and questioned the translation of the original Hebrew version as "sorrow" claiming that the original word really meant "toil" or "labor." Finally Simpson used their own weapon against the clergy.[1]

Simpson pointed out that the first example of using anesthesia to render someone unconscious for a surgical procedure is actually found in the Scriptures. God performed the first anesthetic as He caused Adam to fall into a deep sleep before taking one of his ribs from which to make Eve (Genesis 2:21).

Adam's Rib

Why do you suppose God chose to create Eve from Adam's rib? You would be hard-pressed to find a theological answer for that question. Another frequently asked question that's difficult to answer is: Why did Satan tempt Eve instead of Adam? The answers to both of these questions are found in the treasure box of typology.

In the Scriptures, shortly after the creation of man, we encounter the fall of man. God's intended relationship with humankind was severed. Through typology God then reveals how He will restore that relationship. In order to help us understand the intended relationship, as well as what He would do to mend it, God used symbolism to teach us. The symbolism He chose is very close to our hearts—marriage.

Our Spiritual Bridegroom

John the Baptist was the last of the great prophets to come on the scene. He was the voice crying out in the wilderness to prepare the way for the Christ (Matthew 3:3). He was a prophet of few written words; yet his recorded words were profound. It was his task to point out the Christ; and in doing so John called him the "bridegroom."

John had developed quite a following; the crowds gathered daily to hear him speak and to be baptized. On one occasion, he made an astonishing statement concerning one of the Jews who asked to be baptized: "Look, the Lamb of God, who takes away the sin of the world!" (John 1:29). His meaning was unmistakable. For thousands of years, the Jews had sacrificed innocent lambs for the forgiveness of their sins. John was saying that this man, Jesus of Nazareth, was the *fulfillment of the sacrificial lamb! He must be the Christ!*

From that time on, many Jews began to follow after Jesus instead of John. Some of John's faithful followers came to him one day shortly thereafter and said: "'Rabbi, that man who was with you on the other side of the Jordan—the one you testified about—well, he is baptizing, and everyone is going to him.' To this John replied, 'A man can receive only what is given him from heaven. You yourselves can testify that I said, "I am not the Christ but am sent ahead of him." The *bride belongs to the bridegroom*'" (John 3:26-29, emphasis added).

It is unmistakable that God especially wants us to view Christ as our *spiritual bridegroom*. He sent His Son to betroth us as His bride. If our answer to Him is yes, He will return one day to take us to the heavenly wedding.

The Parable of the Ten Virgins

This truth is explained to us in Jesus' parable of the ten virgins, recorded in the twenty-fifth chapter of the Gospel of Matthew. It is important to note that the term "virgin" here is interchangeable with "potential bride." A potential bride in Jewish culture was assumed to be a virgin because the penalty for premarital relations was death. For example, we are told in Deuteronomy 22:20-21: "If, however, the charge is true and no proof of the girl's virginity can be found, she shall be brought to the door of her father's house and there the men of her town shall stone her to death."

Jesus shares the parable of the ten virgins in the midst of a discussion concerning His Second Coming. In Matthew 24, Jesus is speaking about various signs of the end of the age. He mentions that, "No one knows about that day or hour" (Matthew 24:36). Then He tells the parable of the ten virgins to help us understand what His Second Coming will be like. He says, "At that time the kingdom of heaven will be like ten virgins who took their lamps and went out to meet the bridegroom. Five of them were foolish and five were wise" (Matthew 25:1-2). He then explains what made five of them wise. Verse four tells us: "The wise, however, took oil in jars along with their lamps." In the Scriptures, oil is often used to symbolize the Holy Spirit. For example, the prophets in the Old Testament were anointed with oil symbolizing their anointing with God's Spirit.

The jars represent our physical bodies. The wise virgins, therefore, represent those who have the indwelling of the Holy Spirit. Paul uses similar symbolism in 2 Corinthians 4:7: "But we have this treasure in jars of clay to show that this all-surpassing power is from God and not from us."

Jesus is giving us a word picture of five potential brides who have the indwelling of the Holy Spirit (salvation), and five potential brides who do not. It's as though God has placed a seal on those who have the Holy Spirit to mark them as the ones who will be taken as His bride. "He anointed us, set his seal of ownership on us, and put his Spirit in our hearts as a deposit, guaranteeing what is to come" (2 Corinthians 1:21-22).

At the "midnight cry" when the bridegroom's coming was announced, the foolish virgins asked the wise virgins to share some of their oil; but they were denied. Instead they were told, "Go to those who sell oil and buy some for yourselves" (Matthew 25:9). This passage reveals to us that the Holy Spirit is not something that can be transferred. Salvation is a *personal relationship with the Savior.* One cannot be born into salvation or prayed into salvation! We can tell others where to receive the gift of salvation; yet ultimately every potential bride is responsible to obtain his or her own allotment of oil. We are told in Matthew 25:10-12:

> But while they were on their way to buy the oil, the bridegroom arrived. The virgins who were ready went in with him to the wedding banquet. And the door was shut. Later the others also came. "Sir! Sir!" they said. "Open the door for us!" But he replied, "I tell you the truth, I don't know you."

Several truths are apparent from this parable. First, the kind of relationship God wants to have with us is symbolized by the most intimate, personal relationship known to humanity—*marriage between His Son and us as His bride!*

Second, it is up to us to prepare ourselves and become like the wise virgins. Just as the end of the story reveals: "Let us rejoice and be glad and give him glory! For the wedding of the Lamb has come, and his *bride has made herself ready*" (Revelation 19:7, emphasis added).

Third, there will come a point in time when it will be *too late* to receive Christ as our Savior. The door will be shut and the Bridegroom will say, "I don't know you."

Finally, Jesus ends the parable with His main point: "Therefore keep watch [get yourself ready], because you do not know the day or the hour" (Matthew 25:13).

The Wedding Preparation

"Do you take this woman to be your lawfully wedded wife?" To me, it seems like that question was spoken just yesterday. Even though it took place thirteen years ago, I can remember my wedding day more clearly than I can remember my last birthday. The question seems unnecessary, doesn't it? Why would someone wait until they were asked the key question before saying no? And yet, maybe it is always asked because there is always that possibility.

Can you imagine someone going through all of the necessary expense and preparation to plan a wedding and not go through with it? Some of those preparations include a blood test, sending out invitations, securing the church, arranging for special music, and planning the reception feast. Likewise, why would someone say no to Christ after all He did to prepare for our spiritual wedding day? The blood test was carried out at Calvary, where Christ's blood was shed for the atonement of our sins. Ephesians 2:13 tells us: "But now in Christ Jesus you who once were far away have been brought near through the blood of Christ." The invitations were sent out through thousands of years of prophecy: "As a bridegroom rejoices over his bride, so will your God rejoice over you" (Isaiah 62:5). He literally secured the church by His finished work on the cross: "Christ loved the church and gave himself up for her" (Ephesians 5:25). We get a glimpse of the special music that will accompany us down the heavenly aisle in Revelation 19:6-7: "Then I heard what sounded like a great multitude, like the roar of rushing waters and like loud peals of thunder, shouting: 'Hallelujah! For our Lord God Almighty reigns. Let us rejoice and be glad and give him glory! For the wedding of the Lamb has come, and his bride has made herself ready.'" And concerning the reception we are told, "Blessed are those who are invited to the wedding supper of the Lamb!" (Revelation 19:9).

Another preparation that is typically carried out before the wedding ceremony begins is the wedding portraits. Many pictures are taken to commemorate that special day for the years to come. God has done this for us as well. Throughout the Old Testament Scriptures, God has given us word pictures through prophetic typology to help us more clearly see the marriage of His Son. The first picture in the divine wedding album involves the first union of man and woman. Let's start at the beginning with Adam and Eve.

The First Wedding Picture

Getting back to the question we asked earlier: Why *did* God create Eve from Adam's rib? The answer involves prophetic typology. In 1 Corinthians 15, we find that Paul calls Christ the "last Adam" (verse 45). By using this comparison between Adam and Christ, we can understand the prophetic meaning of the creation of Eve from Adam's rib.

In our analogy, if Adam represents Christ, then Eve would logically represent the bride of Christ—the Church. So how is the Church created or born? The Church is made up of individual Christians. How is one "born" a Christian? Through the atoning blood of Christ that was shed on the cross. If we search the Gospels for the source of the blood Christ shed on the cross, we will discover it did not come from His hands and feet that were nailed to the cross. This makes sense medically because the spikes would have served to plug the holes and prevent the bleeding. Rather, the blood Christ shed on the cross came from His *side*. "One of the soldiers pierced Jesus' side with a spear, bringing a sudden flow of blood and water" (John 19:34). So from Jesus' side (His blood) the bride of Christ (Church) is formed. This was foreshadowed for us in the second chapter of Genesis. Just as Adam's bride was formed from his side, so Christ's bride was formed from the product of His side—His blood!

Continuing with our analogy and our second question—why did Satan tempt Eve instead of Adam? If Adam represents Christ and Eve represents the bride of Christ, then Satan's success would lie with Eve. Satan tried to tempt Christ in the wilderness without success; therefore, he knew he would have to attack the bride of Christ, not Jesus Himself. If partaking of the fruit (from the tree of knowledge of good and evil) represents sin (disobedience to God), then we must realize that Adam did not take the fruit in direct response to Satan's temptation just as Christ did not succumb to any of Satan's temptations. However, notice that Adam did take the fruit *from* Eve. Here we see what Christ would do for His bride. Adam took the sin of his bride upon himself. This is what Christ did on the cross for His bride, the Church. Christ did not sin in the wilderness; but because His bride sinned, He took the sin of His bride upon himself. "God made him who had no sin to be sin for us, so that in him we might become the righteousness of God" (2 Corinthians 5:21).

In the first few chapters of the Scriptures concerning Adam and Eve, God began His wedding album by giving us the foundation of marriage symbolism. As we progress through the Old Testament Scriptures, we encounter more and more prophetic pictures that help us build upon this foundation. We are not given any information concerning the marriages of most of the Old Testament characters; however, we are given a great deal of information about some of the biblical patriarchs and prophets. Why do we have so much information about some of their marriages? I don't believe it is a coincidence. There is a reason why God has given us so many of these details. The Old Testament is not merely a book of history; it is a book of prophecy! In giving us details about the marriages of certain Old Testament characters, God was giving us word pictures about our union with His Son. As we turn the prophetic pages of God's wedding album, the next picture of the Bridegroom upon which we gaze is Isaac.

A Wedding Portrait—Isaac and Rebekah

We discussed in a previous chapter how Isaac was a type of Christ—the child of promise, born through a divine intervention, carried the wood to the place of sacrifice, and willingly allowed himself to be bound for the sacrifice. Now in the twenty-fourth chapter of Genesis, we will see Isaac as a type of Christ once again, this time as the Bridegroom. As the story unfolds, we are told that his father Abraham sent his chief servant back to their land of origin (Aram Naharaim) to acquire a bride for Isaac.

The servant took ten camels loaded with gifts on the journey. When he arrived at his destination, he found Rebekah—the "potential bride." She replied positively to the servant's request for water, and also offered to water his camels. This fulfilled the servant's request to God (he asked for a sign to indicate which woman the Lord had chosen to be Isaac's bride).

After telling Rebekah about his mission to find a bride for Isaac, and informing her family as well, the servant was ready to return with Isaac's bride. But Rebekah's family wanted her to stay. "Then they said, 'Let's call the girl and ask her about it.' So they called Rebekah and asked her, 'Will you go with this man?' 'I will go,' she said" (Genesis 24:57-58). Once again, we see a bride with a choice to make. In Jesus' parable of the ten virgins, each of the potential brides had a choice. It was their decision whether to make themselves ready to be received by the Bridegroom. Five of them chose to prepare wisely by having oil for their lamps; five chose not to make themselves ready.

Another spiritual truth is wrapped up in this story of Rebekah's courtship. We see a picture of the working of the Holy Spirit. The chief servant of Abraham represents the Holy Spirit. Just as the servant sought out the bride for Isaac, one of the tasks of the Holy Spirit is to seek out the bride of Christ by drawing people to a saving knowledge of Jesus Christ! The Spirit beckons us to be the bride of Christ, and like Rebekah, we have a choice to make!

Further, we also see that Rebekah agreed to become the bride of Isaac by *faith*, without first seeing him face-to-face. When she accepted the offer, she was immediately given ten camel loads of gifts! By analogy, when we become the brides of Christ by faith, we too are given gifts—spiritual gifts!

Lastly, we see that after Rebekah agreed to become the bride of Isaac, the chief servant led her through the wilderness to Isaac. The Holy Spirit likewise guides us on our spiritual journey as well. He leads us through the wilderness of this world toward our destination—to Christ, our Bridegroom!

Jacob's Two Wives

The next page of Christ's prophetic wedding album contains a picture of Jacob. In the twenty-ninth chapter of Genesis, we find that Jacob has gone to the same land of Rebekah's origin to acquire his bride (Paddan Aram is another name for Aram Naharaim). His desire was to marry the youngest daughter of his uncle Laban—Rachel; the Scriptures tell us she was very beautiful. Jacob agreed to work seven years for the privilege of her hand in marriage. However, when the seven-year period of work was complete, Laban tricked Jacob and gave his first-born daughter Leah instead. Jacob then agreed to work seven more years to acquire the more desirable hand of Rachel.

Throughout Scripture the number seven is symbolic of completion. So the analogy here is that the completion of the first seven years of work yielded a marriage covenant with the firstborn; the completion of the second seven years resulted in the more desirable covenant with the more beautiful bride. The firstborn bride, Leah, represents the Israelites who were the first covenant people; their marriage is symbolic of the old covenant—the Law. The second time period yielded a more desirable marriage with the bride who was not the firstborn. Rachel represents the new covenant bride of Christ—the Church!

The Kinsman-Redeemer

Our next prophetic portrait is set during the time of the judges: the time sandwiched between when God's people took possession of the Promised Land and their first king was anointed. Throughout the time of the judges, a cycle of events occurred repeatedly. We're told of this cycle in Judges 2:11-19. The Israelites would prostitute themselves by following after the pagan gods of the peoples around them. God's anger would burn against them. After repeated warnings, He would send His judgment upon them. Then the Israelites would cry out to God in repentance; God would raise up a judge to deliver them from their oppression. The Israelites would then have peace and rest during the life of that judge. When the judge died, the people again would turn away from God and serve pagan gods. God would send His judgment upon them, and the cycle would repeat itself.

In the Book of Ruth, we see a picture of Christ as the "kinsman-redeemer." As the book opens, we are told it takes place during the time of the judges and there was a famine in the land. The setting of the story is during a time when the Israelites had been disobedient to God and were under His judgment—a famine. A man named Elimelech took his wife Naomi and their two sons, Mahlon and Kilion, to live in the land of Moab. This act was in disobedience to God. God wanted the Israelites to be a nation set apart from their surrounding nations. He wanted His people to repent and turn to Him when He sent the famines against them—not flee and live among the pagan nations surrounding them!

Mahlon and Kilion took Moabite women to be their wives. God had instructed the Israelites concerning the pagan nations surrounding them:

"Do not intermarry with them. Do not give your daughters to their sons or take their daughters for your sons, for they will turn your sons away from following me to serve other gods, and the Lord's anger will burn against you and will quickly destroy you" (Deuteronomy 7:3-4). With such displays of disobedience to God, we should not be surprised to learn that Elimelech and his two sons perished in the land of Moab!

After the death of her husband and two sons, Naomi hears that in the land of Judah, "the Lord had come to the aid of his people by providing food for them" (Ruth 1:6). She then prepares to return to her homeland where there is food; and according to the Law, provisions must be made for the poor. Leviticus 19:9-10 tells us: "When you reap the harvest of your land, do not reap to the very edges of your field or gather the gleanings of your harvest. Do not go over your vineyard a second time or pick up the grapes that have fallen. Leave them for the poor and the alien." Naomi then proceeds to ask her daughters-in-law, Orpah and Ruth, to remain in Moab. She suggests they find themselves new husbands. Orpah chooses to remain in Moab, but Ruth decides to go with Naomi to Bethlehem.

The Master Artist truly has painted for us a masterpiece in the wedding picture we behold in this story. If God wanted to use these characters as typology, what better way then to make their names significant as well? In the marriage between Elimelech and Naomi we see illustrated the "fall of man." The name Elimelech means "my God is king." Here we see God's intention for humankind—for Him to be our King, our Lord. Naomi means "pleasure." Disobedience is what happens when "my God is king" marries "pleasure." We see illustrated in these characters how the Lord—not pleasure—is to be the focus and center of human attention. In the beginning, Eve disobeyed God and sinned when she confused the two and sought to satisfy her pleasure!

Let's look at what the marriage of Elimelech and Naomi produced. They had two sons—Mahlon and Kilion. The name Mahlon means, "sickly;" Kilion means "wasting away." Can you imagine naming your sons "sickly" and "wasting away"? We are dealing with typology here; God is speaking volumes through the names of these characters!

Furthermore, when Naomi returned to Bethlehem, she requested that she not be called Naomi anymore. "'Don't call me Naomi,' she told them. 'Call me Mara, because the Almighty has made my life very bitter'" (Ruth 1:20). When "my God is king" marries "pleasure," the end result is always—sickliness and wasting away, which is eventually followed by bitterness and death!

The names of the two daughters-in-law are significant as well. The name Orpah means "fawn." A fawn is a young deer; however, an additional, seldom-used definition is "to show fondness."[2] Fondness speaks of a superficial love, rather than a deep, sincere love. Orpah was "fond" of Naomi and her God but not sincere or dedicated. When thoughts of the difficult road ahead—living in a foreign land with no man to provide for her— became a reality, she chose to go back to her old ways and stay with her own people and pagan gods.

The name Ruth, on the other hand, means "beauty." In Ruth we see a picture of the beauty of true and sincere faith. She didn't know what lay ahead in Bethlehem; but she had faith in the unseen God of Israel and made the decision to trust in Him. "'Look,' said Naomi, 'your sister-in-law is going back to her people *and her gods.* Go back with her.' But Ruth replied, 'Don't urge me to leave you or to turn back from you. Where you go I will go, and where you stay I will stay. Your people will be my people *and your God my God*'" (Ruth 1:15-16, emphasis added).

Once they were settled in Bethlehem, Naomi sent Ruth to glean in the fields of her relative. While working one day, Ruth met a man named Boaz who was a relative of her father-in-law, Elimelech. As the story unfolds, Ruth finds favor in Boaz's eyes, and Boaz makes preparations to provide for her. She eventually informs Boaz that he is a "kinsman-redeemer" for her. According to the Law, a kinsman-redeemer was a close relative who was obligated to take in the widow of a deceased kinsman (Deuteronomy 25:5-10).

Boaz, however, informs Ruth that there was a relative closer than himself; that man had the first right to be her kinsman-redeemer. Boaz then meets the unnamed kinsman-redeemer and proposes that this man should redeem the land and property of Elimelech. At first he agrees to redeem Elimelech's land and property, until Boaz informs him that in doing so he would also acquire Ruth, the Moabitess, as his wife! "At this, the kinsman-redeemer said, 'Then I cannot redeem it because I might endanger my own estate. You redeem it yourself. I cannot do it'" (Ruth 4:6). His answer doesn't make much sense. He was ready to redeem the property until he found out he would have to take Ruth as his bride. As we said earlier, Deuteronomy 7:3-4 forbade the marrying of foreign women. What doesn't make sense is why Boaz was able to marry Ruth if the other kinsman-redeemer could not?

Again, God is telling us something through prophetic typology. Boaz means "strength." As the kinsman-redeemer, Boaz foreshadows Christ, who took us as His Gentile bride. He paid the price to redeem us through His shed blood on the cross. In Boaz we see a picture of the "strength" of salvation.

What does the nearer kinsman-redeemer represent? He had the first opportunity to redeem Ruth, the Gentile bride; yet he could not do it. He represents the Law. The Law came first and had the first opportunity to redeem mankind. But as Paul explains:

> Clearly no one is justified before God by the law, because, "The righteous will live by faith"... Christ redeemed us from the curse of the law by becoming a curse for us... He redeemed us in order that the blessing given to Abraham might come to the Gentiles through Christ Jesus, so that by faith we might receive the promise of the Spirit. (Galatians 3:11,13a,14)

Therefore, Boaz did what *the Law did not allow*—he took for himself a Gentile bride! Similarly, Christ did what the Law could not do and fulfilled the meaning of the kinsman-redeemer. He took for himself a Gentile bride—the Church!

Once the unnamed kinsman-redeemer refused to redeem the land and property that had belonged to Elimelech, Boaz agreed to become the redeemer:

> Then Boaz announced to the elders and all the people, "Today you are witnesses that I have bought from

> Naomi all the property of Elimelech, Kilion and Mahlon. I have also acquired Ruth the Moabitess, Mahlon's widow, as my wife." (Ruth 4:9-10a)

Ruth became Boaz's bride and an heir of his estate! However, notice that Boaz redeemed the land and property belonging to Kilion (Orpah's husband) as well. Don't miss this extremely important point! Boaz redeemed Kilion's widow too. The story ends with a description of the descendants of Boaz and Ruth. Ruth became an ancestor of King David and eventually even Christ Himself!

But what of Orpah? We are told nothing more about her. When she made her decision not to follow after the God of Israel and went back to her old way of paganism, she missed out on the entire inheritance offered by Boaz, her kinsman-redeemer. She was never heard from again! She therefore represents those who reject Christ's offer to become their spiritual kinsman-redeemer. She foreshadows the "foolish virgins" who do not ready themselves to receive their heavenly bridegroom and therefore have no share in His inheritance.

In the story of Ruth, God gives us a picture of the strength of salvation that is offered through our kinsman-redeemer—Jesus Christ. We also learn that we all have a choice. One potential bride chose to follow after the God of Israel and was received by her kinsman-redeemer; the other chose to follow after pagan gods and was never mentioned in the Bible again. Just like in the parable of the ten virgins, we potential brides have a choice to make as well. We can choose pleasure as our priority and experience only a fondness for Christ—or we can follow Him with passion and sincerity as we prepare for His coming! If we choose to follow Christ, He will do what the Law could not do and take us as His redeemed bride!

Boaz had the right to take Ruth as his bride because of his bloodline. He was a blood relative of Elimelech and was therefore a potential kinsman-redeemer. So by analogy, what gave Christ the right to take the church as His bride? The answer is found in the next wedding picture of the Bridegroom—the story of David and Goliath.

The Victory of Our Champion

The story of David and Goliath is a popular children's Bible story. Children are taught that if you put your faith in God, He will give you victory over the "giants" in your life. That is a wonderful truth, and it needs to be bestowed upon today's youth; yet what is the deeper meaning of the story? What is God trying to tell us? Why would an entire nation stake everything on the outcome of a battle between two men? Why would Saul allow a boy to represent the entire nation of Israel when the stakes were so high? The answers to these questions are found in the treasure box of typology.

"Be careful what you ask for because you just might get it!" Those words, so often spoken by an old friend of mine, seem to echo one of the lessons that God is teaching His people as they face the Philistine army with Goliath poised in the foreground. What had the nation of Israel asked for? Let's take a look: "So all the elders of Israel gathered together and came to Samuel at Ramah. They said to him, 'You are old, and your sons do not walk in your ways; now appoint a king to lead us, such as all the other nations have'" (1 Samuel 8:4-5).

The Israelites wanted a king to rule over them so they could be like all the other nations. It seems, however, that God did not want His people to have a king over them. He wanted them to put their trust in Him to deliver them from their enemies, not in an earthly king. This becomes evident as we continue: "But when they said, 'Give us a king to lead us,' this displeased Samuel; so he prayed to the Lord. And the Lord told him: 'Listen to all that the people are saying to you; it is not you that they have rejected, but *they have rejected me as their king*'" (1 Samuel 8:6-7, emphasis added).

In their demand for a king to rule over them, we are given insight into their motivation—their heart. The Israelites were rejecting God as their ruler! Samuel's attempt to reason with them fell on deaf ears: "But the people refused to listen to Samuel. 'No!' they said. 'We want a king over us. Then we will be like all the other nations, with a king to go before us and fight our battles'" (1 Samuel 8:19-20). Amazing! They were the chosen, privileged nation of God; yet they wanted to be like everybody else! So God gave them just what they asked for. He allowed them to crown Saul as their king; then God provided an opportunity for Saul to go before them and fight their battle.

The story unfolds with the Israelites positioned on one hillside while the Philistines were positioned across the Valley of Elah on another hillside. This was a "battle of championship"—a concept that was foreign to the Israelites. This type of contest was of Aegean origin, an area from which the Philistines are thought to have migrated. Edward E. Hindson explains in his book, *The Philistines and the Old Testament*:

> Goliath challenged the army of Israel to select a champion from their ranks to confront him in a battle of championship. The single combatants would decide the fate of each army. The individual victor would bring victory to his army and the loser would cause his people to go into slavery. He defied Israel to send forth her man but all of the Israelites were afraid. If anyone were to answer this challenge, it should have been newly-elected King Saul, the leader of Israel who stood "head and shoulders above any man in Israel" (1 Samuel 9:2).[3]

The Israelites had asked for a king to fight their battles, but Saul did not answer the challenge. They placed their trust in an earthly king and now God had given them what they asked for. Hindson further explains:

> Such a practice of one man representing an entire army was unheard of among the Semitic peoples who believed in the corporate unity of the nation in battle."[4]
>
> "The concept of such a battle was based upon the Philistine concept of religion. To the Philistines a battle of champions would test the favor of the gods. If the gods could give the champion victory, they could give the entire army victory. Therefore, the test of the conflict was a test of the power of the gods.

This explains why Goliath made a mockery of the god of the Israelites (See 1 Samuel 17:43).[5]

How could Saul let David, a young shepherd boy, represent the entire nation of Israel? Saul allowed David to engage Goliath in battle because it was a battle of the gods! Saul, it seems, had a spiritual problem. The one prerequisite for a champion was that the Lord be with him! So how did Saul know the Lord was with David? "One of the servants answered, 'I have seen a son of Jesse of Bethlehem who knows how to play the harp. He is a brave man and a warrior. He speaks well and is a fine-looking man. *And the Lord is with him*'" (1 Samuel 16:18, emphasis added).

How could Saul be *sure* that the Lord was with David? When Saul expressed his doubts about sending the boy to fight, David recounted for Saul how he killed a lion and a bear with his bare hands. David reassured Saul by saying, "The Lord who delivered me from the paw of the lion and the paw of the bear will deliver me from the hand of this Philistine" (1 Samuel 17:37).

What is God trying to tell us with this story about the battle between David and Goliath? The Philistines were the enemies of God's people. Their champion, Goliath, therefore represents the leader of the enemies of God's people—Satan.

Meanwhile, God's people put their trust in a man—Saul, their king—to deliver them from their enemies. Their trust, however, was misplaced. Saul could not give them victory. The battle was a test of the power of God! God taught the Israelites to place their trust in Him, not man! It was a hard lesson to learn.

David, on the other hand, was God's chosen one; he was anointed by Samuel in the preceding chapter. As God's chosen anointed one, David is a representation of Christ. The word *Christ* literally means "anointed one."

Realizing this, we see how the battle of championship represents a foreshadowing of the conflict between Christ and Satan. There are many parallels between the two stories: For *forty days* Goliath tempted Israel to send forth their champion, just as Satan tempted Christ in the wilderness for forty days; David's victory over Goliath gave

God's people victory over the enemy, just as Christ's victory over Satan did the same for all believers; and finally, the champion who defeated Goliath was promised a great reward.

First Samuel 17:25 reveals: "The king will give great wealth to the man who kills [Goliath]. He will also give him his daughter [Michal] in marriage." By analogy, we can answer our earlier question: What gave Christ the right to take the church as His bride? Just as David defeated Goliath and won the right to take his bride, so Christ's defeat over Satan allowed Him to take the church as His bride!

The Undeserving Bride

Our last portrait of the Bridegroom comes from the Book of Hosea. When God called Hosea to be His prophet, He asked him to do a strange thing: "When the Lord began to speak through Hosea, the Lord said to him, 'Go, take to yourself an adulterous wife'" (Hosea 1:2). Why would God ask Hosea to marry an adulterer? As the story unfolds, Hosea obediently marries Gomer and they have three children. Sometime after the third child was born, Gomer left Hosea and went back to being a prostitute.

The Lord then made another request of Hosea: "The Lord said to me, 'Go, show your love to your wife again, though she is loved by another and is an adulteress. Love her as the Lord loves the Israelites, though they turn to other gods and love the sacred raisin cakes.' So I bought her for fifteen shekels of silver and about a homer and a lethek of barley" (Hosea 3:1-2). The fact that the Lord asked Hosea to buy Gomer back as his bride (even though she was unfaithful to him) is unthinkable to us; but here we see a foreshadowing of what Christ would do to acquire us as His bride. Many times throughout the Old Testament Scriptures, the Israelites were called an "adulterous people" when they were disobedient to God. Christ came to acquire us as His bride, even though we are also an adulterous people. "But God demonstrates his own love for us in this: *While we were still sinners*, Christ died for us" (Romans 5:8, emphasis added). He paid the price to *redeem* us or buy us back as His bride. As the apostle Paul explains, "You are not your own; you were bought at a price" (1 Corinthians 6:19-20). Just as Hosea paid the price to acquire his adulterous bride, Christ has come to pay the price to acquire us as His bride. And what a price He paid!

Our Spiritual Proposal

God indeed performed the first anesthetic procedure when He caused Adam to fall into a deep sleep before removing one of his ribs from which to make Eve. He performed that operation to bring about the first marriage between a bridegroom and his bride. In doing so, God foreshadowed for us the birth of the Church through the great price that Jesus paid—His shed blood on the cross. Once He developed the foundation of the marriage symbolism with Adam and Eve, God then built upon that foundation throughout the Old Testament Scriptures.

The story of how Isaac married Rebekah tells us of the workings of the Holy Spirit in obtaining Christ's bride. Jacob's fourteen years of service to Laban reveals to us the new covenant relationship we have because of Christ's finished work. Boaz's betrothal of Ruth speaks volumes about our redemption by Christ as our kinsman-redeemer. David's victory over Goliath foreshadows for us that Christ's victory over Satan secured His right to take the church as His bride. The story of Hosea reassures us that even though we may be an undeserving, adulterous bride, Christ still paid the price to redeem us.

John the Baptist hailed Christ as the fulfillment of Old Testament prophecy concerning the Bridegroom. And Christ enlightens us, through His parable of the ten virgins, that if we are "wise virgins" and make ourselves ready by having the oil of the Holy Spirit in our "jars," we will indeed be taken to the very "wedding feast of the Lamb."

The preparations have been made. Christ has secured the Church. He has sent the invitations and passed the blood test. All that is left is our answer to the key question: "Will you take this Savior as your *gracefully* wedded Bridegroom?" A wedding feast has been prepared for those who will say "yes" to our Lord's spiritual proposal.

— CHAPTER SEVEN QUESTIONS —

1. John the Baptist said, "The bride belongs to the bridegroom."
   a. How does one become the bride of Christ?
   b. Do you believe that the "potential bride" has any choice in the matter? (Consider Matthew 25:1-13, Genesis 24:57-58, and Revelation 19:7 as you formulate your answer.)

2. Review the Jewish betrothal custom described earlier in the discussion of the Feast of Trumpets contained in Chapter 5, "The Fall Feasts." How does the betrothal custom apply to Christ as our spiritual bridegroom?

3. Review the many preparations that Jesus made for His spiritual wedding day. Can you think of any other preparations that He made?

4. Explain how each of the following Old Testament characters revealed prophetic information about the bride of Christ:
   a. Eve
   b. Rebekah
   c. Rachel
   d. Ruth
   e. Michal
   f. Gomer

5. The author describes the Old Testament types of the bridegroom as a "divine wedding album." What other Old Testament characters might have their portraits in this wedding album?

6. Joseph (Genesis 41:45) and Moses (Exodus 2:21) both acquired a Gentile bride before the time of plagues upon Egypt.
   a. Could they serve as a type of our spiritual bridegroom?
   b. What might their actions say about the timing of the rapture of the Church?

7. Consider Rebekah being led by the "chief servant" through the wilderness toward her betrothed bridegroom.
   a. Can you make a comparison to the wilderness journey of God's people after the Exodus?
   b. The "chief servant" and the "pillar of fire" (Genesis 13:21) represent the leading of the Holy Spirit. How does God's Spirit lead His bride today?

JOSHUA

Choose for yourselves this day whom you will serve...But as for me and my household, we will serve the Lord.
—*Joshua 24:15*

*I*t wasn't supposed to end this way," echoed through my mind as I watched him die. It was the last night of my medical school tenure. The next morning I would leave through the doors of the medical center for the last time as a medical student.

The patient I was grieving over was a man named Arthur. Two years earlier, Arthur had been the subject of my family history assignment while I was rotating on the Family Practice service. Back then I had an opportunity to meet with him and his wife in their home and learn about their lives together, as well as Arthur's illness—end stage emphysema.

Arthur's condition was the result of a bad decision that he'd made many years earlier—to smoke cigarettes. After years of allowing destructive forces to work upon his lungs, he was dependent upon continuous supplemental oxygen and spent almost as much time in the hospital as he did at home.

Arthur had become a very special person to me and because of our relationship, I knew he did not want to be placed on a respirator! He knew his lungs were so deteriorated that if he were to be placed on a respirator, he would never be able to come off of it! The respirator would just prolong his suffering.

So a few weeks before Arthur died I was shocked when I stumbled across a bed in the medical intensive care unit with Arthur's last name on it. The patient connected to the respirator was indeed my friend Arthur! How could this have happened? He had not wanted to be placed on a respirator. As I talked with his wife, I learned the answer. In the heat of the moment, when she was asked, "Do you want us to do everything we can?" she consented to the respirator.

For several weeks, I could only watch as Arthur suffered and finally succumbed to the consequence of the choice he had made so many years before. If only children and teenagers could learn from Arthur's mistake and avoid making the same tragic mistake that resulted in his suffering and eventual death!

A Bad Choice at Kadesh Barnea

My anguish over the suffering and death of one so dear to me was probably mirrored by the Israelites as they watched their loved ones suffer and die in the wilderness! The reason for their suffering and death was a bad decision they had made years earlier at a place called Kadesh Barnea!

During their journey to the Promised Land, God had done everything for the Israelites and provided for their every need. He freed them from bondage in Egypt, parted the Red Sea before them, drowned the Egyptian army, supplied manna for them to eat and water from the rock for them to drink. He eventually led them to the border of the land He had promised to their forefathers as their inheritance.

Now it was time for the Israelites to make a choice. Twelve spies had been selected; each one was a leader from his respective tribe. The spies spent forty days scouting out the Promised Land. They reported to the people that the land did indeed "flow with milk and honey" as God had promised. However, there was a problem. Giants lived there—the "descendants of Anak" (Numbers 13:28).

Of the twelve spies, Caleb and Joshua stood alone and recommended: "We should go up and take possession of the land, for we can certainly do it" (Numbers 13:30). But the rest of the spies reported: "We can't attack those people; they are stronger than we are" (Numbers 13:31). The Israelites then "grumbled" against the Lord and His appointed leaders—Moses and Aaron. They *made a decision* not to enter into the Promised Land as God had intended. It was their choice! Instead, they rejected Moses and Aaron as their leaders and planned to stone Joshua and Caleb! Because of their decision, God brought His judgment upon them:

> As surely as I live, declares the Lord, I will do to you the very things I heard you say: In this desert your bodies will fall—every one of you twenty years old or more who was counted in the census and who has grumbled against me. Not one of you will enter the land I swore with uplifted hand to make your home, except Caleb son of Jephunneh and Joshua son of Nun. (Numbers 14:28-30)

A Test of Faith

The Israelites had been given a *test of their faith*—they failed miserably! When they decided they could not defeat the giants living in the Promised Land, they were really saying, "God can't give us the victory." How quickly they had forgotten what God did for them. The Israelites couldn't free themselves from bondage in Egypt. They couldn't part the Red Sea or provide for their needs in the wilderness. *God did those things!* Likewise, they couldn't defeat the giants in the Promised Land—but God could! They needed to rely on God to provide a great victory over the inhabitants of the Promised Land. Instead, because they lacked the faith to rely on God, He caused them to wander in the wilderness for forty years—one year for each of the forty days the spies spent exploring the Promised Land. God confined them to the wilderness for forty years, until everyone who was twenty years of age or older at Kadesh Barnea died there!

Joshua and Caleb were the only two over the age of twenty, out of the two million members of that generation, who exhibited a true faith in God and were allowed to enter into the Promised Land! The proof that this was a test of their faith is found in God's castigation:

"Your children will be shepherds here for forty years, suffering for your *unfaithfulness*, until the last of your bodies lies in the desert" (Numbers 14:33, emphasis added).

A Legacy of Faith

The ten unfaithful spies were described in the Scriptures as *leaders*. Each was the leader of an entire tribe. Their names were: Shammua, Shaphat, Igal, Palti, Gaddiel, Gaddi, Ammiel, Sethur, Nahbi, and Geuel. Do you recognize any of their names? I would be floored if you did! As I type them on my computer, every one of them has a red line underneath because my computer doesn't recognize them either! They left no legacy. Time has forgotten them and you probably will too by the time you finish this chapter!

On the other hand, the two faithful spies have quite a legacy. Parents still name their children Caleb and Joshua. My son, Joseph, has a best friend named Joshua; I have a nephew named Caleb. Isn't it interesting that the two names that are remembered thousands of years later are those who exhibited a true faith in God! I don't believe it's a coincidence that of the twelve "leaders" who scouted out the Promised Land, the only ones whose names have been memorialized are the two who had a true faith in God!

Commander of the Army of the Lord

After the forty years ended and the unfaithful generation perished in the wilderness, God once again brought the Israelites to the border of the Promised Land. This time they were located on the east bank of the Jordan River, just across from Jericho. On this occasion God sent a special messenger to give His word to Joshua.

> Now when Joshua was near Jericho, he looked up and saw a man standing in front of him with a drawn sword in his hand. Joshua went up to him and asked, "Are you for us or for our enemies?"
>
> "Neither," he replied, "but as commander of the army of the Lord I have now come." (Joshua 5:13-14)

Who was this "commander of the army of the Lord"? I believe it was none other than Jesus Christ Himself! Just as we saw in an earlier chapter, "The Lamb of God," Christ sometimes appeared in the Old Testament as the Angel of the Lord to give His personal touch to the Master's work. The Angel of the Lord stopped Abraham from sacrificing Isaac so that we could know that God Himself intended to provide the Lamb. Here the Angel of the Lord is revealing to us that the battle belongs to Him! It is Christ who will win the victory—our part is faith!

Why do I believe the Commander of the army of the Lord and the Angel of the Lord were actually the Lord Jesus Christ? First, notice Joshua's response: "Then Joshua fell facedown to the ground in reverence, and asked him, 'What message does my Lord have for his servant?' The commander of the Lord's army replied, 'Take off your sandals, for the place where you are standing is holy'" (Joshua 5:14-15). This was the same thing that the Angel of the Lord said to Moses from the burning bush (Exodus 3:5).

He was also described as "standing...with a drawn sword in his hand" (Joshua 5:13). This is similar to a description of the Angel of the Lord whom Balaam encountered: "Then the Lord opened Balaam's eyes, and he saw the angel of the Lord standing in the road with his sword drawn" (Numbers 22:31).

This messenger from God was a "theophany" or a pre-incarnate appearance of Christ. Warren Wiersbe points out in his book, *Be Strong*: "This paragraph records one of the pre-incarnate appearances of the Lord Jesus Christ recorded in the Old Testament. To Abraham the pilgrim, the Lord came as a traveler to share in a friendly meal (Gen. 18:1-8). To Jacob the schemer, He came as a wrestler to bring him to the place of submission (32:24-32). The three Hebrew men met Him as their companion in the furnace of fire (Dan. 3:25), and Joshua met Him as the Captain of the Lord's armies."[1]

When we understand that the Commander of the army of the Lord was a pre-incarnate appearance of Christ, His answer to Joshua's question becomes interesting. Joshua asked, "Are you for us or for our enemies?" His reply was "neither." Surely Christ was on the side of the Israelites. After all, He gave Joshua the plans to defeat Jericho. What is God telling us through this dialogue? God does not take sides. God is for all peoples. "God so loved the *world* that he gave his one and only Son, that *whoever* believes in him shall not perish but have eternal life" (John 3:16, emphasis added).

The Big Picture

God was orchestrating the events in the battle of Jericho so that through the prophecy of typology, we could have a better understanding of Him and his purposes. And once again we see the Angel of the Lord was present and giving His personal touch to the Master's artistry. Let's take a look at the message God orchestrated through the types and shadows given to us in the life of Joshua.

The Promised Land

The Promised Land is symbolic of our spiritual inheritance. Some have equated the Promised Land as typical of heaven. Wiersbe points out for us however, "The Book of Joshua records battles, defeats, sins, and failures—none of which will take place in heaven."[2] The Promised Land is, therefore, not a good representation of heaven; but it is a type of our spiritual inheritance! Although not representative of heaven, it is a picture of God's gracious intention for us—our spiritual life. Spiritual life doesn't begin when one goes to heaven; it begins when we receive Christ as our Savior and are given the indwelling of His Holy Spirit. At that moment we become spiritual beings—that is, Christ lives in us. Therefore, our spiritual inheritance involves our spiritual life, which begins the moment we are saved and continues on into heaven. After we are saved, we still have battles, defeats, sin, and failure. So while the Promised Land is not symbolic of heaven, it is symbolic of our spiritual life. It represents where God wants us to be.

Moses

As the Book of Deuteronomy draws to a close, we learn that Moses wasn't going to be allowed to lead the children of Israel into the Promised Land. God explains to Moses, "This is because…you broke faith with me in the presence of the Israelites at the waters of Meribah Kadesh in the Desert of Zin and because you did not uphold my holiness among the Israelites" (Deuteronomy 32:51).

So what horrible act did Moses commit at Meribah Kadesh? The Israelites had quarreled against Moses because there was no water for them there and Moses cried out to God on behalf of the people:

> The Lord said to Moses, "Take the staff, and you and your brother Aaron gather the assembly together. Speak to that rock before their eyes and it will pour out its water." So Moses took the staff from the Lord's presence, just as he commanded him. He and Aaron gathered the assembly together in front of the rock and Moses said to them, "Listen, you rebels, must *we* bring you water out of this rock?" Then Moses raised his arm and struck the rock twice with his staff. Water gushed out, and the community and their livestock drank. (Numbers 20:7-11, emphasis added)

So we see Moses' great failure—instead of giving God the glory for the miracle of bringing water from the rock, Moses took the credit!

Wasn't his punishment a bit harsh? After all, Moses faithfully went to Egypt and confronted Pharaoh. He faithfully led the Israelites through the wilderness for forty years and put up with their grumbling and begged God to spare their lives more than once. To us, his punishment seems out of proportion for his crime. Especially when you consider that before the Exodus, Moses killed an Egyptian and fled to Midian. Even then, God was still willing to use him to deliver the Israelites from Egypt. So why won't God allow him to enter the Promised Land now!

Looking at the big picture through the lens of typology, we can understand what God was telling us by His decision to deny Moses entrance into the Promised Land. If the Promised Land represents our spiritual inheritance (where God wants us to be), what does Moses represent? Moses represents the Law. The first five books of the Old Testament are known as the Books of Moses or the Books of the Law. God is, therefore, teaching us that just as the Israelites couldn't get to their Promised Land by following Moses (the Law), we can't get to our spiritual inheritance by following the Law either! "Know that a man is not justified by [following] the Law, but by faith in Jesus Christ" (Galatians 2:16). Something else is required.

Joshua

Moses wasn't allowed to enter the Promised Land, so the Israelites needed another leader to follow. God ordained Joshua as their new leader to follow. If Moses represents the Law, what does Joshua represent? Joshua represents for us a type of Christ. The name Joshua is the Hebrew equivalent to the Greek name Jesus. The two names literally mean "The Lord is Salvation." God chose a new leader for His people to follow to their symbolic spiritual inheritance—and his name was equivalent to the name of our Lord and Savior—Jesus! God certainly stated His message plainly through His orchestration of these typical events. By God's divine orchestration, we are given a portrayal of Galatians 2:16. We can't get to our spiritual inheritance, our Promised Land, by following the Law. We can only get there through faith in Jesus Christ!

The Jordan River

The barrier that kept the Israelites from entering where God intended them to be was the Jordan River. What might this body of water represent? The Hebrew word for Jordan means "descent" giving us a clue as to its prophetic role. I believe the Jordan is symbolic of the "descent" of man or the "fall" of man, if you will.

When Adam and Eve sinned against God, mankind was thereafter separated from dwelling in the presence of God. That event is often called "the fall of man." If the Jordan River (the descent) represents the barrier that separates mankind from dwelling where God originally intended, then we should not be surprised that the Jordan ends in a body of water known as the Dead Sea. The Dead Sea is so named, because it is just that—dead. There is nothing alive there from the animal or plant kingdom! It sustains no life of any kind. What an appropriate description!

The "descent" of man, unless crossed, will result in spiritual death. "Cross" is the key word here. By following Joshua, the Israelites were able to cross over the Jordan. By what Jesus did on the cross, we are able to follow Him and cross over our sin barrier that separates us from dwelling in the presence of God!

It is also interesting to note that when God parted the Jordan River, "the water from upstream stopped flowing. It piled up in a heap a great distance away, at a town called Adam" (Joshua 3:16). How fitting that the barrier that is symbolic of the fall of man was backed up at a town called Adam—the one with whom the fall of man began!

Caleb

Caleb and Joshua were the only two, of all the Israelites over the age of twenty, who were allowed to enter into the Promised Land. Therefore, if Joshua symbolically represents Christ, whom does Caleb represent?

The Hebrew word for Caleb literally means "dog." It turns out that the Israelites commonly referred to the Gentiles as dogs. For example, a Greek woman came and begged Jesus to heal her daughter. Jesus replied: "'First let the children eat all they want,' he told her, 'for it is not right to take the children's bread and toss it to their *dogs*.' 'Yes, Lord,' she replied, 'but even the *dogs* under the table eat the children's crumbs'" (Mark 7:27-28, emphasis added). Because of her faithful reply, Jesus healed her daughter.

Maybe Caleb symbolically represents the Gentiles who one day would be allowed to enter into the symbolic fulfillment of the Promised Land—because of their faith in following Christ!

Another Test of Faith

Forty years had elapsed since the Israelites failed their first test of faith, which resulted in their death in the wilderness. Now we have the next generation gathered at the edge of the Promised Land once again. However, they had their own test of faith awaiting them. Just as there had been twelve men selected to scout out the Promised

Land forty years earlier, twelve men were now selected for this new test of faith. "Now then, choose twelve men from the tribes of Israel, one from each tribe. And as soon as the priests who carry the ark of the Lord—the Lord of all the earth—set foot in the Jordan, its waters flowing downstream will be cut off and stand up in a heap" (Joshua 3:12-13).

The Scriptures further inform us: "The Jordan is at flood stage all during harvest" (Joshua 3:15). Their test was to step into the Jordan while it was at flood stage. Why was this a test? In the Focus on the Family video series "That the World May Know: Faith Lessons," Ray Vander Laan points out that the geography of the Jordan was such, that at the point where they would have stepped in, they would have been stepping in over their heads! So God asked them to step into (over their heads) a raging river at flood stage!

Another factor to consider is that these Israelites had been brought up in the desert for forty years. The one thing the desert lacks most is water. Therefore, there is a high probability that these Israelites couldn't swim! This then, was their test of faith. God would part the Jordan only *after* their feet touched the water. They had to rely upon Him to save them!

This time, however, they passed the test. "As soon as the priests who carried the ark reached the Jordan and their feet touched the water's edge, the water from upstream stopped flowing" (Joshua 3:15-16). And so the Israelites successfully passed their test of faith and finally entered their Promised Land!

The Defeat of Jericho

After crossing the Jordan River, the Israelites' next challenge was to defeat the walled city of Jericho. This could only be accomplished by precisely following the instructions they received from the Commander of the Lord's army! He commanded them to march around the city each day for six days; then on the seventh day, they were to march around Jericho seven times. On that last day, after the seven trips around Jericho, they were to blow their trumpets and give a great shout. This was, needless to say, an incredibly unorthodox way to attack an enemy city! It was indeed, another test of faith. Only when they had followed the Lord's instructions completely did the walls of Jericho fall down and the enemy was defeated.

It is interesting to note the significance of the trumpet blasts. For the Israelites (children of God), the trumpet blasts brought victory; for the enemies of God, the trumpet signaled their defeat and destruction! The blast of the trumpet foreshadows a Second Coming event of Christ. Trumpets play a prominent role in the events of the Tribulation. "For the Lord himself will come down from heaven, with a loud command, with the [shout] of the archangel and with the trumpet call of God" (1 Thessalonians 4:16).

It is at the trumpet blast announcing His Second Coming that Christ will deliver His people to heaven, but for His enemies there will be destruction! "The great day of the Lord is near—near and coming quickly…That day will be a day of wrath, a day of distress and anguish, a day of trouble and ruin, a day of darkness and gloom, a day of clouds and blackness, a day of *trumpet* and battle cry against the corner towers. I will bring distress on the people and they will walk like blind men, because they have sinned against the Lord" (Zephaniah 1:14-17, emphasis added).

Rahab Is Spared

The battle of Jericho has an interesting twist to it. Rahab was a Gentile prostitute who lived in a dwelling that was incorporated into one of the walls of the city. When Joshua sent two spies into Jericho, Rahab hid them and saved their lives. As a result, when Jericho was destroyed she and her household were spared. She was told to place a "scarlet cord" in the window of her dwelling. All who were there with her in her home when the city was sieged would be spared the destruction that the Lord brought upon Jericho.

There is a similarity between Rahab's salvation and the Exodus Passover. Just as the Israelites were commanded to place the scarlet blood of the lamb over the entrance to their dwellings in order to escape the destruction brought by the Lord, Rahab was to place a scarlet cord over her window. The scarlet cord and the blood of the lamb were both a foreshadowing of the blood of Christ, which also allows us to escape the judgment of God!

Why was Rahab spared? She was, after all, a Gentile—and a prostitute at that! She did aid the spies; but that was only part of the reason she was spared. What would motivate her to help the spies? On closer examination, we find that Rahab possessed a genuine faith in God. Listen to her profession of faith: "The Lord your God is God in heaven above and on earth below" (Joshua 2:11).

Therefore, since the destruction of Jericho foreshadows the time of the Tribulation, Rahab might symbolically represent those who will believe and have faith in Christ during the Tribulation. "After this I looked and there before me was a great multitude that no one could count, from every nation, tribe, people and language, standing before the throne and in front of the Lamb.... *These are they who have come out of the great tribulation;* they have washed their robes and made them white in the blood of the Lamb" (Revelation 7:9, 14, emphasis added).

Faith — A Choice

As Joshua was nearing the end of his days, he gave the Israelites a final challenge. His departing words seem to echo a reoccurring theme throughout his life: "Choose for yourselves this day whom you will serve, whether the gods your forefathers served beyond the River, or the gods of the Amorites, in whose land you are living. But as for me and my household, we will serve the Lord" (Joshua 24:15).

The Israelites had a choice to make. They could choose to have faith in God or they could serve the pagan gods who were not gods at all. The ten spies at Kadesh Barnea chose not to have faith in God and have been forgotten. The Israelites chose to follow the advice of the ten spies and perished in the wilderness. On the other hand, Joshua, Caleb, Rahab, and the second generation of Israelites chose to have faith in God and were allowed to dwell in the Promised Land.

We face the same choices. Joshua's final challenge extends from ancient days to us today. We have a choice to make. We must either choose to have a saving faith in Jesus Christ—the only way for us to cross over into the Promised Land (our spiritual inheritance)—or we will choose to serve the gods of this world, which are not gods at all! My friend, Arthur, said many times that he wished he could go back and undo his decision to smoke tobacco. But for Arthur, there is no going back. He realized the right choice too late to make a difference in his life. As a consequence, he underwent much suffering. I can imagine the Israelites during their forty years of wandering in the wilderness echoing Arthur's remarks. For them, it was also too late to prevent their suffering and death. Joshua, a type of Christ, challenges us from the pages of Scripture to choose the Lord. Our final destination depends upon our choice. We can chose to follow Christ and (like those Israelites who followed Joshua) enter into our spiritual inheritance or chose a path (like my friend Arthur) that leads to suffering and death.

— CHAPTER EIGHT QUESTIONS —

1. At Kadesh Barnea, Joshua and Caleb stood against the majority
    and recommended that the Israelites enter and take possession of
    the Promised Land. (Numbers 14)
    a. As you consider the culture that we live in today, if you
        choose to follow God's Word would you be in the majority
        or in the minority?
    b. What are some issues that would put you in opposition to
        the majority if you were true to following God's Word in our
        culture today?

2. Now that you have finished the chapter and are answering the
    questions:
    a. Can you remember the names of any of the ten unfaithful
        spies?
    b. Other than Joshua and Caleb, how many other names can
        you think of that are memorialized from the Old Testament
        Scriptures?

3. Review the geographical symbolism involved as Joshua led his
    people into the Promised Land. Explain the significance of the
    following:
    a. Wilderness
    b. Jordan
    c. Promised Land
    d. Dead Sea
    e. Town of Adam

4. Consider Joshua's interaction with the "commander of the army
    of the Lord."

a. Who do you believe the "commander of the army of the Lord" was?

b. What is the significance of his answer to Joshua's question, "Are you for us or our enemies?"

5. How was Joshua a type of Christ? Consider the following:
   a. His name
   b. His position
   c. His receiving instructions from the Lord
   d. His crossing over the Jordan

6. How was Rahab a type for Christians? Review Joshua 2:1-21, 6:17 and answer the following:
   a. Her faith
   b. Her courage
   c. Her commitment
   d. Her obedience
   e. The scarlet cord
   f. Her salvation during the destruction of Jericho

ZAPHENATH-PANEAH

*But God sent me ahead of you to preserve for you a remnant on
earth and to save your lives by a great deliverance.*
—Joseph (Genesis 45:7)

*I*t was on a cold night in November 1895 when the accident
happened. Professor Roentgen had been experimenting with
an apparatus that, unknown to him, caused the emission of
x-rays as a by-product. Accustomed to his darkened laboratory, he
observed that whenever the apparatus was working, a chemical-coat-
ed piece of cardboard lying on the table glowed with a pale green
light. When he placed his hand between the source of the beam and
the lighted cardboard, he could see the bones inside his fingers within the shadow of his hand.[1]

That "accidental" viewing of the bony shadow of the professor's
hand would change the future of medicine forever. Thanks to
Roentgen, the field of radiology was born and countless individuals
have reaped the benefits of his accidental finding. Radiographs allow
us to see beyond the surface to the deeper subsurface areas of our
anatomy, revealing information that would have gone unnoticed
without them.

As we illuminate details in the lives of specific Old Testament
characters, we too might be as surprised as Roentgen by the shadows
that we find. Getting a glimpse beyond the surface, we may discov-

er information foreshadowing Christ that otherwise may have gone unnoticed. Clearly none of the Old Testament personalities were a perfect type of Christ, in and of themselves; they all had flaws. But God was able to use various aspects of their lives to allow us a partial prophetic glimpse of Christ's shadow.

Jonah, for example, was certainly not a perfect type of Christ. He ran from God! It was only after he suffered God's punishment that he reluctantly delivered God's message to Nineveh. Then he became angry because his mission was successful and the people repented! He certainly was not representative of the attitude of Christ. Yet we know Jonah was a partial type of Christ because Jesus explained that Jonah's three days in the belly of the fish foreshadowed the three days that He would spend in the tomb (Matthew 12:40).

In modern medicine one of the most detailed radiographic views of the subsurface anatomy is provided by computed tomography (CT) scans. Technically, this is done by moving both the x-ray tube and the film around the patient during the exposure. They are moved about a pivot point calculated to fall in the plane of the object to be studied. In this way the shadows of all the structures not in the plane selected for study are intentionally blurred because they move relative to the film.[2] The CT scan is then able to provide a cross-sectional view of the subsurface anatomy. In this way it becomes possible to study multiple cross-sections and produce a more detailed three-dimensional view of the subject.

In our study of the Old Testament personalities, if we allow them to be our pivot point and move our examining lens around their lives, we will find that many of them are CT's (Christ Types). As a Christ Type, they give us a "cross-view" of the future! That is, information concerning the One who would hang on the cross. However, each character provides only a partial cross-view of Christ's shadow. The more cross-views we are able to obtain, the clearer the true image of Christ's shadow will be for us to see. While each of the Old Testament character types reveal some information about Christ, none provides as complete a representation of the life of Christ as Joseph. Arthur Pink points out:

As we read thoughtfully the books of the Old Testament our study of them is but superficial if they fail to show us that in divers ways and by various means God was preparing the way for the coming of His Son. The central purpose in the Divine Incarnation, the great outstanding object in the life and death of the Lord Jesus, were prefigured beforehand, and ought to have been rendered familiar to the minds of men. Among the means thus used of God was the history of different persons through whom the life and character of Christ were to a remarkable degree made manifest beforehand. Thus Adam represented His headship, Abel His death, Noah His work in providing a refuge for His people. Melchizedek pointed to Him as priest, Moses as prophet, David as king. But the fullest and most striking of all these typical personage was Joseph, for between his history and that of Christ we may trace fully a hundred points of analogy![3]

Radiologists examine CT scans by first studying an overview of the area and then progressing to a more detailed examination one cross-sectional frame at a time. The information obtained from each cross-sectional view is then assimilated and combined to provide a three-dimensional view of the anatomy. Why don't we approach the Old Testament character of Joseph as a radiologist would? Let's start with an overview, and then focus our attention on one cross-view frame at a time.

Joseph the Patriarch and Joseph of Nazareth

Backing up and approaching the life of Joseph with a bird's eye view, we first might wonder if was merely a coincidence that the earthly father of Jesus was also named Joseph. Consider the following passage:

Because Joseph her husband was a righteous man and did not want to expose her to public disgrace, he had in mind to divorce her quietly. But after he

had considered this, an angel of the Lord appeared
to him *in a dream* and said, "Joseph *son of David*, do
not be afraid to take Mary home as your wife,
because what is conceived in her is from the Holy
Spirit." (Matthew 1:19-20, emphasis mine)

An angel of the Lord appeared in a dream to Joseph of Nazareth
and revealed to him that a miracle would come to pass. His betrothed
bride Mary would give birth to a child; through that child, God would
provide salvation for humankind. But why did the angel address
Joseph by the title "son of David"? David was not the name of Joseph's
father. We need look back only four verses to see that in the genealogy of Jesus, Joseph is said to be the son of Jacob. Anyone else would
have addressed Joseph by his common title—Joseph son of Jacob. In
addressing Joseph as the son of David, the angel was referring to his
lineage from the ancestry of King David. The angel was subtly telling
Joseph that he would be the earthly father of the Christ, in fulfillment
of Isaiah 9:7: "He [Christ] will reign on David's throne and over his
kingdom, establishing and upholding it with justice and righteousness
from that time on and forever."

These events in the lives of Mary and Joseph were foreshadowed in
the life of Joseph the Patriarch many hundreds of years before. He too
was the son of Jacob. He too received a message from God in a dream.

Joseph's dream, as recorded in Genesis 37:1-11, was two-fold. In
the first, his eleven brothers' sheaves of grain bowed down to his
sheaf. The second dream had a similar theme, in which the sun,
moon, and eleven stars also bowed down to him. The two dreams
foretold the future time when Joseph would rise to a position of
power in Egypt and his family would come and bow before him. His
dream was foreshadowing the time when Joseph would save his people from perishing in the midst of a great famine.

Using his dreams, God was foretelling Joseph the patriarch information that was very similar to the message Joseph of Nazareth
received. So as we consider both Josephs, we see a parallel message.
Both Josephs, sons of Jacob, received a message from God in a dream
telling them that they would play a role in a great miracle, which

would result in the salvation of their people. In Joseph the patriarch's situation, God provided a miracle that allowed a Hebrew slave to rise from an Egyptian prison to become Pharaoh's right-hand man. Concerning Joseph of Nazareth, God allowed him to be the earthly caretaker of the Christ-child. He too would go to Egypt in order to protect Jesus from Herod and ultimately provide for his people the means of salvation. Joseph the Patriarch would provide salvation for his people from a great famine by becoming the caretaker of the grain of Egypt. Joseph of Nazareth would be the caretaker of the Christ-child, the "bread of life." Jesus also was brought out of Egypt and would offer salvation from spiritual famine for all humanity.

Joseph the Patriarch Foreshadows Christ

Now that we have studied the overview, we can focus on the first cross-view and examine the deeper details. We first stumble across Joseph the patriarch's similarity with Christ in that there is a scarcity of information concerning their early years. We're told: "Joseph, being seventeen years old, was feeding the flocks with his brethren; and the lad was with the sons of Bilhah, and with the sons of Zilpah, his father's wives: and Joseph brought unto his father their evil report" (Genesis 37:2, KJV). We read nothing of Joseph's early childhood. He is seventeen years old when we are first introduced to him. Likewise, as we read the Gospels' portrayal of the life of Christ, there is a scarcity of information concerning His childhood years as well. Aside from His visit to the temple on Passover at the age of twelve (Luke 2:41- 52), we are told nothing of His life until the beginning of His ministry at the age of thirty.

Further, as we are introduced to Joseph, we learn that he was a shepherd. He was "feeding the flocks." It would be difficult to overlook the fact that God desires that we behold His Son as our Shepherd. David put it most beautifully in Psalm 23:1, "The Lord is my shepherd, I shall not be in want." Jesus Himself reassures us: "I am the good shepherd. The good shepherd lays down his life for the sheep" (John 10:11).

Another point we should note is that Joseph's brothers, who were mentioned in this passage when he brought his father an "evil report," were only his half-brothers. They were the sons of Jacob's wives—Bilhah and Zilpah. Joseph's mother was Rachel. Likewise, the Jews to whom Jesus was sent were only His half-brothers. Jesus had a different Father—God.

Finally, we learn in verse two that Joseph testified to his father that his half-brothers' actions were "evil." We are told three reasons why Joseph's brothers hated him: because of his testimony concerning their evil deeds, his dreams concerning the future, and his father's love for him. The Scriptures tell us: "And they hated him all the more because of his dream and what he had said" (Genesis 37:8). This reminds us of the unjust hatred Jesus had to endure because of His "evil report," "The world cannot hate you, but it *hates* me because *I testify that what it does is evil*" (John 7:7, emphasis added).

The next cross-view that we will study involves a dream:

> Joseph had a dream, and when he told it to his brothers, they hated him all the more. He said to them, "Listen to this dream I had: We were binding sheaves of grain out in the field when suddenly my sheaf rose and stood upright, while your sheaves gathered around mine and bowed down to it…" Then he had another dream, and he told it to his brothers. "Listen," he said, "I had another dream, and this time the sun and moon and eleven stars were bowing down to me." (Genesis 37:5-7, 9)

Through his two dreams, Joseph was able to foretell the time when he would rise to a position of power in Pharaoh's court and consequently provide for the needs of his people in their time of famine. Jesus also foretold of a time when He would provide for the needs of His people: "In my Father's house are many rooms; if it were not so, I would have told you. I am going there to prepare a place for you" (John 14:2).

The two-fold nature of Joseph's dreams foreshadows for us the two-fold nature of the sovereignty of Christ. The "field" speaks of Jesus' earthly domain. The prophet Zechariah writes, concerning the earthly millennial reign of Christ, "The Lord will be king over the whole earth. On that day there will be one Lord, and his name the only name" (Zechariah 14:9). In the other dream, "the sun, moon, and eleven stars" speak of Christ's heavenly sovereignty. In the Gospel of Matthew we read: "Then Jesus came to them and said, 'All authority in heaven and on earth has been given to me'" (Matthew 28:18).

God Sent His Son

Now let's examine a cross-view that reveals for us God's purpose in sending His Son as the Incarnate—that is, God in human form.

> Now his brothers had gone to graze their father's flocks near Shechem, and Israel said to Joseph, "As you know, your brothers are grazing the flocks near Shechem. Come, I am going to send you to them." "Very well," he replied. So he said to him, "Go and see if all is well with your brothers and with the flocks, and bring word back to me." Then he sent him off from the Valley of Hebron. (Genesis 37:12-14)

Here we see that Joseph's brothers were apart from their father; we can draw a parallel between their condition and that of mankind. We cannot help but see the concern of Jacob for his sons. So much so that he sent his most beloved son Joseph to those who were far away from his presence. Likewise, since the time of the fall of man in the Garden of Eden, humanity has been separated from dwelling in the presence of God. Realizing that God is orchestrating the events in the life of Joseph for our understanding, we begin to comprehend the great love and concern that God has for those who, because of sin, are far off from His presence. "For God so loved the world that he gave his one and only Son" (John 3:16).

Also significant is Joseph's response to his father's request to go and check on the well being of his brothers. Joseph must have known about his brothers' hatred of him and that he would not be well received by them; yet his reply to his father's request is immediate and without reservation: "'Very well,' he replied." We gain insight not only into God the Father's love for humanity, but also the love of Christ as well. Jesus willingly and without reservation came to seek out those who were lost. He willingly paid the price for their atonement. Jesus Himself explained: "The Son of Man came to seek and to save what was lost" (Luke 19:10). And further He said: "I lay down my life—only to take it up again. No one takes it from me, but I lay it down of my own accord" (John 10:17-18).

In His parable of the lost sheep, as recorded in Luke 15:1-7, Jesus gives us insight into the fervor by which He came to seek those who are lost and separated from their heavenly Father. The owner's willingness to leave the ninety-nine in order to seek after the one who was lost, and the rejoicing that occurs when it was found, is a picture of Christ's love and earnest search for those who are lost.

And just as Joseph had to seek out his brothers *where they were located*, the Word had to become flesh and dwell among us (*where we are located*). What an incredible irony—*the one through whom all was created allowed Himself to be created* in order to "seek and to save what was lost!"

Joseph left the Valley of Hebron to seek out his brothers who were supposed to be at Shechem; but he did not find them there. He discovered they had moved on to Dothan. The names of the locations in this narrative are significant as well. Hebron, where Joseph departed from, means "fellowship" or "alliance." We are therefore given a picture of the fellowship Jesus had among the Trinity in heaven, yet He willingly left to seek His lost brethren.

We are first introduced to Shechem (where Joseph's brothers were supposed to be) in the twelfth chapter of Genesis. At God's request Abram obediently left his home country of Haran for Shechem, in the land of Canaan. It was at Shechem that God made a covenant with Abram and promised him the land of Canaan for his descendants. Shechem, therefore, represents for us the promise of God as a reward for obedience to His Word. Joseph's brothers were *supposed* to be at Shechem; but on their own accord, they had moved to Dothan. Arthur Pink explains it this way:

"Dothan" signifies "Law or Custom." And it was there Jesus found His brethren, dwelling under the bondage of the Law, and slaves to mere religious formalism. Yes, the Law of Jehovah had degenerated into the "customs" of the Pharisees. "Laying aside the commandments of God, ye hold the traditions of men" (Mark 9:8), was our Lord's charge against them.[4]

This perfectly foreshadows for us the condition in which Jesus found His brethren when He tabernacled among them. They should have been receiving God's promises based on their obedience to His Word; instead, they were slaves to man-made laws and traditions. Their condition prompted God's prophetic admonition of them: "These people come near to me with their mouth and honor me with their lips, but their hearts are far from me. Their worship of me is made up only of rules taught by men" (Isaiah 29:13).

Rejection of the Son

Next in our story we see that Joseph's own brothers sold him as a slave:

> Judah said to his brothers, "What will we gain if we kill our brother and cover up his blood? Come, let's sell him to the Ishmaelites and not lay our hands on him; after all, he is our brother, our own flesh and blood." His brothers agreed. So when the Midianite merchants came by, his brothers pulled Joseph up out of the cistern and sold him for twenty shekels of silver to the Ishmaelites, who took him to Egypt. (Genesis 37:26-28)

This foreshadows for us when Jesus was betrayed and sold out by one of His own disciples. Just as Joseph was sold as a slave, Judas sold Jesus out for thirty pieces of silver, which happens to be the price of a slave. Arthur Pink further points out: "Is it not exceedingly striking to note that from among the twelve sons of Jacob *Judah* should be the one to make this horrible bargain, just as from the twelve apostles *Judas* (the Anglicized form of the Greek *equivalent*) was the one to sell the Lord!"[5]

Temptation and False Accusation

Now let's take a closer look at the cross-view concerning the temptations and false accusations against Christ. Joseph had prospered in Egypt and had been placed in charge of the household of his master:

> Now Joseph was well-built and handsome, and after a while his master's wife took notice of Joseph and said, "Come to bed with me!" But he refused...And though she spoke to Joseph day after day, he refused to go to bed with her or even be with her. One day he went into the house to attend to his duties, and none of the household servants was inside. She caught him by his cloak and said, "Come to bed with me!" But he left his cloak in her hand and ran out of the house...She kept his cloak beside her until his master came home. Then she told him this story: "That Hebrew slave you brought us came to me to make sport of me. But as soon as I screamed for help, he left his cloak beside me and ran out of the house." When his master heard the story his wife told him, saying, "This is how your slave treated me," he burned with anger. Joseph's master took him and put him in prison, the place where the king's prisoners were confined. (Genesis 39:6b-8a, 10-12, 16-20a)

In Joseph's temptation we see that although he was repeatedly tempted, he did not succumb to the tempter. This foreshadows for us the temptations of Christ. Though Satan repeatedly tempted Christ in the wilderness, Jesus did not sin. The writer of Hebrews explains: "For we do not have a high priest who is unable to sympathize with our weaknesses, but we have one who has been tempted in every way, just as we are—yet was without sin" (Hebrews 4:15).

We also see that Christ, like Joseph, was falsely accused. We are told: "The chief priests and the whole Sanhedrin were looking for false evidence against Jesus so that they could put him to death. But they did not find any, though many false witnesses came forward" (Matthew 26:59-60). It's amazing that, as far as we can tell from the Scriptures, Joseph utters no opposition to the false accusation that was made about him. As we read the text, Joseph remains silent before his accuser, foreshadowing for us the silence of Christ before His accusers: "Then the high priest stood up and said to Jesus, 'Are you not going to answer? What is this testimony that these men are bringing against you?' But *Jesus remained silent*" (Matthew 26:62-63, emphasis added).

Standing before the one who would falsely judge Him, Jesus, the perfect "Lamb of God," was silent in fulfillment of Isaiah 53:7: "He was oppressed and afflicted, yet he did not open his mouth; he was led like a lamb to the slaughter, and as a sheep before her shearers is silent, so he did not open his mouth."

The Cross Foreshadowed

Look closely at the next cross-view and see if you can find a portrait of Jesus on the cross:

> Pharaoh was angry with his two officials, the chief cupbearer and the chief baker, and put them in custody in the house of the captain of the guard, in the same prison where Joseph was confined...
>
> After they had been in custody for some time, each of the two men—the cupbearer and the baker of the king of Egypt, who were being held in prison—had a dream the same night, and each dream had a meaning of its own...
>
> Then Joseph said to them, "Do not interpretations belong to God? Tell me your dreams."
>
> So the chief cupbearer told Joseph his dream. He said to him, "In my dream I saw a vine in front of me, and on the vine were three branches. As soon as

it budded, it blossomed, and its clusters ripened into grapes. Pharaoh's cup was in my hand, and I took the grapes, squeezed them into Pharaoh's cup and put the cup in his hand."

"This is what it means," Joseph said to him. "The three branches are three days. Within three days Pharaoh will lift up your head and restore you to your position, and you will put Pharaoh's cup in his hand, just as you used to do when you were his cupbearer"...

When the chief baker saw that Joseph had given a favorable interpretation, he said to Joseph, "I too had a dream: On my head were three baskets of bread. In the top basket were all kinds of baked goods for Pharaoh, but the birds were eating them out of the basket on my head."

This is what it means," Joseph said. "The three baskets are three days. Within three days Pharaoh will lift off your head and hang you on a tree. And the birds will eat away your flesh."

Now the third day was Pharaoh's birthday, and he gave a feast for all his officials....He restored the chief cupbearer to his position, so that he once again put the cup into Pharaoh's hand, but he hanged the chief baker, just as Joseph had said to them in his interpretation. (Genesis 40:2-3, 4b-5, 8b-13, 16-20, 21-22)

Joseph's confinement with the cupbearer and the baker foreshadows Jesus' incarceration on the cross. Luke 23:32-33 tells us: "Two other men, both criminals, were also led out with him to be executed. When they came to the place called the Skull, there they crucified him, along with the criminals—one on his right, the other on his left."

Joseph made remarkable predictions about Pharaoh's two officials. He predicted that one would perish but the other would be saved and restored to his position in the kingdom. After three days, Joseph's predictions came true—the cupbearer was restored to his position of service to the king and the baker lost his life!

What a foreshadowing of the events that transpired while Jesus hung on the cross! Jesus made a similar prediction concerning the fate of the two men who were crucified alongside Him:

> One of the criminals who hung there hurled insults at him: "Aren't you the Christ? Save yourself and us!" But the other criminal rebuked him. "Don't you fear God," he said, "since you are under the same sentence?" ...Then he said, "Jesus, remember me when you come into your kingdom." Jesus answered him, "I tell you the truth, today you will be with me in paradise." (Luke 23:39-40, 42-43)

One of the criminals believed in Christ; because of his profession of faith, Jesus declared that he would be with Him in heaven that very day. What an incredible experience it must have been for this man! One moment he was a condemned criminal, justly given the death penalty; the next moment, he was a child of God in heaven! He had done nothing to deserve his salvation—as none of us can do. He simply placed his faith in Christ. It was all he could do. In the end, his profession was all that was needed. He received the same fate as the cupbearer—he was saved and allowed to take his position as a servant in the Kingdom. What an incredible picture of God's amazing grace!

What must we do to one day receive our place in the Kingdom? Our answer is found in Paul and Silas' response to the Philippian jailer who asked the same question: "Believe in the Lord Jesus, and you will be saved" (Acts 16:31).

What about the fate of the other criminal who was crucified with Christ? He is foreshadowed by the baker, who Joseph predicted would lose his life. What prediction did Jesus make concerning the fate of the other criminal? It is obvious from his sarcastic remarks that he did not believe Jesus was the Christ. Jesus' prediction of his fate was the same given to all who refuse to believe on Him: "Whoever does not believe will be condemned" (Mark 16:16).

Let us not pass over this passage too quickly and miss several other prophetic details. Both the cupbearer and the baker's fates were sealed after three days. Jesus spent three days in the tomb then arose victoriously, sealing the fate of those who place their faith in Him.

What significance can we find in the occupations of these two officials? The cupbearer (who was saved from death) had the job of holding the king's cup of wine. As we discovered in chapter three, "Spiritual Sustenance," wine may be symbolic of the blood of Christ. He reveals the symbolic meaning of the wine at the Last Supper when He says, "This cup is the new covenant in my blood, which is poured out for you" (Luke 22:20). Therefore, by analogy, if we are cupbearers of Christ (bearers of the blood of the Lamb), like the chief cupbearer of Pharaoh we too will be restored to our position in the kingdom.

What can we infer from the baker's occupation? Baking was done over a flame or in an oven. It reminds us of the eternal destiny of those who, like the unbelieving criminal on the cross, will not believe. Jesus said:

> As the weeds are pulled up and burned in the fire, so it will be at the end of the age. The Son of Man will send out his angels, and they will weed out of his kingdom everything that causes sin and all who do evil. They will throw them into the fiery furnace, where there will be weeping and gnashing of teeth. (Matthew 13:40-42)

The Ascension to the Throne

Pharaoh had a dream and his counselors were unable to interpret its meaning. The cupbearer then remembered that Joseph had correctly interpreted his dream, and he conveyed this information to Pharaoh. Joseph subsequently was called before Pharaoh, where he revealed to him the meaning of his dream. He explained that the dream involved seven years of abundance, followed by seven years of severe famine. Pharaoh was so pleased with the counsel of Joseph that he was appointed second in command over all the land of Egypt!

> Then Pharaoh said to Joseph, "Since God has made all this known to you, there is no one so discerning

and wise as you. You shall be in charge of my palace, and all my people are to submit to your orders. Only with respect to the throne will I be greater than you."... Then Pharaoh said to Joseph, "I am Pharaoh, but without your word no one will lift hand or foot in all Egypt." Pharaoh gave Joseph the name Zaphenath-Paneah and gave him Asenath daughter of Potiphera, priest of On, to be his wife. (Genesis 41:39-40, 44-45a)

Here we see that Joseph ascended from his lowly place in prison to sit at the right hand of the most powerful person on the face of the earth—Pharaoh himself! Likewise, Jesus arose from the prison of death and ascended to take His place at the right hand of the most powerful one in the universe—God the Father!

Joseph was given the name "Zaphenath-Paneah" by Pharaoh, which aside from the name of Pharaoh was the name above every name in the land. How perfectly this foreshadows the risen Christ. "Therefore God exalted him to the highest place and gave him the name that is above every name" (Philippians 2:9). The name "Zaphenath-Paneah" means "Sustainer of Life." Even the name itself speaks volumes about our risen Lord.

Finally, let's not overlook the marriage of Joseph to his Gentile bride, Asenath, before the time of the famine. Once he arose from prison to sit at the right hand of the king, received the name that was above every other name, and became the "Sustainer of Life," Joseph acquired his Gentile bride. The fulfillment of this foreshadowing is found in the Church. After Jesus arose from the prison of death to sit at the right hand of the Father, was given the name that is above every name, and became the "Sustainer of Life," He acquired the Gentile Church as His bride. Assuming that you, the reader, are a Christian, I will presume that no one has ever told you that you were prophetically represented by Asenath, daughter of Potiphera, priest of On!

It is also significant to note that Joseph acquired his bride *before* the famine came upon Egypt. We see a parallel with the life of Moses as he acquired a Gentile bride *before* the plaques came upon Egypt

(Exodus 2:21). I believe that the famine and plaques may represent the time of the tribulation. If this is the case, then the taking of the Gentile bride *before* the famine gives support to the church being raptured *before* the tribulation.

Our Savior

Our last cross-view involves Christ's desire for our lives. As Joseph had predicted, the seven years of plenty were followed by seven years of famine. During the years of famine, Joseph sold grain to the people until they had no more money with which to buy grain. Then he gave them grain in exchange for their livestock. When there was no more livestock with which to obtain grain, Joseph gave them grain in exchange for their land until all of their land was under his control. He then *purchased the people* in exchange for his provision.

> When that year was over, they came to [Joseph] the following year and said, "We cannot hide from our lord the fact that since our money is gone and our livestock belongs to you, there is nothing left for our lord except our bodies and our land...."
>
> Joseph said to the people, "Now that I have bought you and your land today for Pharaoh, here is seed for you so you can plant the ground...."
>
> "You have saved our lives," they said. "May we find favor in the eyes of our lord." (Genesis 47:18, 23, 25)

What this accomplished was that all men were now equal. What an incredible plan God gave him! There were no divisions between rich and poor, no hierarchy with regard to possessions or property. All men were equal and they no longer had anything to rely upon for security—except Joseph. And Joseph met their needs, as evidenced by their proclamation, "You have saved our lives," they said. "May we find favor in the eyes of our lord."

Here we see the desire of Christ for our lives. He paid the price on the cross to purchase us. As Paul reminds us: "You are not your own; you were bought at a price" (1 Corinthians 6:19). All people are equal before the Lord. He doesn't want humankind depending on wealth, possessions, or property; He wants us to rely completely and solely upon Him to provide for our needs! He wants to be the Lord of our lives! We too should proclaim: "You have saved us, may we find favor in the eyes of our Lord."

Professor Roentgen's discovery of his bony shadow was an accident. He had no idea that it would change the course of medicine and play a vital role in saving lives. But the shadows of Christ that God has provided in the life of Joseph the patriarch were no accident! God carefully orchestrated the events in order to reveal information about His Son who would change the course of humankind and provide the way for salvation. From the ancient pages of Scripture, Jesus speaks to us through Joseph, "But God sent me ahead of you to preserve for you a remnant on earth and to save your lives by a great deliverance" (Genesis 45:7).

— CHAPTER NINE QUESTIONS —

1. Review the genealogy of Jesus found in Matthew 1:1-16.
   a. Who is mentioned as the father of Joseph?
   b. Why do you believe the angel of the Lord addressed Joseph as "Joseph son of David"? (Matthew 1:20)
   c. Was Jesus born through a pure Jewish lineage? (Take a look at the women mentioned in Matthew 1:5.) What does this reveal about the purpose of the Messiah?

2. God revealed prophetic information to Joseph the patriarch through dreams. Review the dreams of the following Old Testament characters. What prophetic information did God reveal through their dreams?
   a. Abraham (Genesis 15:12-21)
   b. Jacob (Genesis 28:10-15)
   c. Daniel (Daniel 7)

3. Read Genesis 37:12-18. If God wanted to use the events in the life of Joseph as a foreshadowing of Christ, explain the significance of the following details in the narrative:
   a. Joseph
   b. Israel
   c. Dothan
   d. Shechem
   e. Hebron
   f. The sons of Bilhah and Zilpah
   g. Joseph's response "Very well"
   h. "They plotted to kill him"

4. Read the account of Joseph's incarceration found in Genesis 40. If the events are a foreshadowing of Christ:
   a. Who does the Pharaoh represent?
   b. Who does the baker foreshadow?

   c. Who does the cupbearer foreshadow?

   d. What is the significance of the "three days"?

5. Read of Joseph's ascension to power in Genesis 41:39-45. How could information about Christ be foreshadowed by the following quotes?

   a. "God has made all this known to you"

   b. "You shall be in charge of my palace"

   c. "all my people are to submit to your orders"

   d. "the name Zaphenath-Paneah"

   e. "Asenath...to be his wife"

6. Consider Joseph's remarks to his brothers, "You intended to harm me, but God intended it for good to accomplish what is now being done, the saving of many lives" (Genesis 50:20).

   a. Does this verse imply that God was orchestrating these events?

   b. How does this verse foreshadow Christ?

   c. Is there similarity to the words spoken by Jesus while on the cross?

THE VOW OF THE NAZIRITE

So was fulfilled what was said through the prophets: "He will be called a Nazarene." — Matthew 2:23b

On my graduation day from medical school, I participated in a long-standing ritual at the commencement ceremony—reciting the Oath of Hippocrates. Around the nation thousands of graduating medical students stood and repeated the following words:

> I swear by Apollo, the Physician, by Aesculapius, by Hygea, by Panacea and by that which I hold most sacred that according to my ability I will keep this, my Oath and Covenant:
>
> With purity and holiness I will pass my life and practice my art.
>
> As I labor in the Temple of Healing, my first thoughts will be the life, happiness and health of my patients. To this end I will try to treat my brethren in this art as I wish them to treat me.
>
> I will use my power to heal my fellow man to the best of my judgment; I will abstain from harming or wronging any man by it.
>
> I will maintain the utmost respect for human life from the time of its inception.
>
> Into whatever houses I enter I will go into them for the benefit of my patients. Whatever in professional

practice I see or hear in the lives of men which should not be spoken abroad I will not divulge.

For the sake of the sick I will pursue knowledge of this art throughout the days of my life. With eagerness I will learn from my brothers, and humility I will share my knowledge with them. In respect for those who have led me into the paths of Medicine, I will lead those who follow me.

Should I transgress these promises may my soul know no peace, but while I keep this oath inviolate, may it be granted to me to enjoy life and the practice of the art, forever honored by all men.

Try and imagine thousands of soon-to-be doctors standing and swearing by Aesculapius, Hygea, and Panacea. Most of them had no clue who those characters were. Regardless of that fact, it is a commendable oath. Contained within the Oath of Hippocrates is the desire to live one's life with purity and holiness; the desire to place the interests of one's patients first; the Golden Rule; a respect for human life; the importance of confidentiality; and the yearning to learn and teach others. In a day when there seems to be an assassination of standards and morals, it is encouraging that the medical profession initiates its neophytes with such a commendable standard by which to practice their art.

Did God ever offer an oath for His people to live by? Certainly the Bible is the ultimate standard for how we are to live our lives. But what about during the Old Testament period—before the entire Bible was written? Did God ever provide an opportunity by which His people could take an oath to live by a higher standard? I know what you are thinking. Sure, God gave His people the Ten Commandments to live by. That is true; but those were *commandments*, not oaths. They were not optional. All of God's people were required to obey them. What about an oath that is both optional and goes beyond the standard commandments of God? Not everyone is called upon to take the Oath of Hippocrates, for example. Only those who are willing to devote themselves to the practice of medicine are asked to take the oath. Was there an oath that God ordained for those who were willing to devote themselves to a deeper commitment in following after God? I believe there was. It is found buried in the Books of the Law, specifically the Book of Numbers. It is called the Vow of the Nazirite.

The Vow of the Nazirite

When I first read the details about this vow, I was initially struck by its name. Why "Nazirite"? In the first four chapters of Numbers, there are more "ites" than you can shake a stick at. There were the Levites, Gershonites, Kohathites, Merarites, and Amramites, just to name a few. Basically you take the name of a descendant of Jacob, and add "ite" to it; now you've got the name of a clan. The clan of Reuben was called the Reubenites, for example. So then who was Nazir, from whom we get the term "Nazirite"?

Search if you will; but I don't believe you will find anyone named "Nazir" listed. So why Nazirite?

Maybe the name Nazirite comes from a location or a town. Could it be a reference to the town of Nazareth? I don't believe so because God's people were still in the wilderness—they had not yet made it into the Promised Land where the town of Nazareth is located. Furthermore, the town of Nazareth probably wasn't founded until hundreds of years after the time of the wilderness wanderings of God's people. So back to our original question: Why was it called the Vow of the Nazirite?

Perhaps it was prophecy. Consider the following verse concerning Christ: "So was fulfilled what was said through the prophets: 'He will be called a Nazarene'" (Matthew 2:23b). This passage is contained within a narrative concerning Joseph's return from Egypt with Mary and Jesus after the death of King Herod. Joseph decided to settle and raise Jesus in the town of Nazareth. So Matthew is saying that because Nazareth was Jesus' hometown, He would be called a Nazarene, as was foretold by the prophets. But the question then becomes: Where in the Old Testament Scriptures do the prophets make that prophecy? It is perplexing; if you do a word search of the Old Testament Scriptures, you will not find the word "Nazarene."

So what was Matthew talking about? Was he perhaps referring to the passage in the Book of Numbers concerning the Vow of the Nazirite?

Let's look at this from a different angle. Why was Jesus called a Nazarene anyway? I know He was from Nazareth; but if He had been from Midian, He would have been called a Midianite. If He had been from Edom, He would have been called an Edomite. So why wasn't He called a Nazirite? Maybe it had something to do with the Vow of the Nazirite. You see, the Vow of the Nazirite was a part of the Torah—the Hebrew Law. It was well known to the Jews of His day. If someone from Nazareth had been called a Nazirite, people might have misunderstood and thought they had taken this vow. So if someone pointed to Christ and said, "There is Jesus the Nazirite," they may have mistakenly thought that Jesus had taken the Vow of the Nazirite. Could it be then, that the reason Jesus was called the Nazarene, instead of the Nazirite, was to avoid confusion between the city and the vow? Is it possible then, that the prophecy that Matthew referred to was the Vow of the Nazirite passage from Numbers 6?

I believe that the Vow of the Nazirite passage was a prophecy concerning Jesus the Nazarene and foreshadows what is expected of us if we vow to follow Him. Allow me to explain why.

Our Vow of Commitment

We first must understand that Jesus did *not* take the Vow of the Nazirite. This is clear from the Gospels' portrayal of His life. He drank wine and had contact with dead bodies—both of which were forbidden to a Nazirite. Therefore, the vow isn't about Christ; it is about those who vow to be committed to Christ.

When in our lives do we make a vow? We make a vow on our wedding day when we pledge to be committed to our spouse. How appropriate it is that this oath was referred to as a "vow." When we accept Christ as our Savior, we become His spiritual bride and He becomes our spiritual Bridegroom. We are betrothed to Him until the day when the heavenly angelic choir sings: "Hallelujah! For our Lord God Almighty reigns. Let us rejoice and be glad and give him glory! For the wedding of the Lamb has come, and his bride has made herself ready" (Revelation 19:6b-7).

As the betrothed bride of Christ, we have certain commitments that are expected of us. The Vow of the Nazirite foreshadows these expectations.

The Conditions of the Vow

Let's take a closer look at the conditions of this vow. It is important to point out from the outset that this vow was voluntary. No one was ever *required* to take this vow. It was *available to everyone who desired to take it*, but it was not forced on anyone. Much the same as salvation is completely voluntary. It is available to *everyone* but not forced on anyone: "This is good, and pleases God our Savior, who wants *all men* to be saved and to come to a knowledge of the truth" (1 Timothy 2:4, emphasis added).

Additionally, the Vow of the Nazirite was equally available to both men and women. In Hebrew Law, there was a disparity between men and women in their worship of God. Women were not allowed to be priests or to participate in certain aspects of worship. However, with respect to the Vow of the Nazirite, there was no difference between men and women. The Scriptures tell us: "The Lord said to Moses, 'Speak to the Israelites and say to them: "If a *man or woman* wants to make a special vow, a vow of separation to the Lord as a Nazirite, he must...""" (Numbers 6:1-3, emphasis added).

Likewise, with regard to salvation, there is no difference between men and women. Paul explains: "You are all sons of God through faith in Christ Jesus, for all of you who were baptized into Christ have clothed yourselves with Christ. There is neither Jew nor Greek, slave nor free, *male nor female*, for you are all one in Christ Jesus" (Galatians 3:26-28, emphasis added).

Separated unto God

The intent of the vow was for the individual to be separated for the purpose of being holy to the Lord. It was a special vow, a "vow of separation." Concerning the Nazirite it was said, "He must be holy until the period of his *separation* to the Lord is over" and "throughout the period of his *separation* he is consecrated to the Lord" (Numbers 6:5, 8, emphasis added). Here we see the meaning of sanctification. The word *sanctified* means to be set apart—to be separate. Paul tells us "It is God's will that you should be sanctified…. For God did not call us to be impure, but to live a holy life" (1 Thessalonians 4:3, 7).

We are to be separate from the world for the purpose of living holy. Our instructions for living a holy life of sanctification are summarized in Romans 12:1: "Therefore, I urge you, brothers, in view of God's mercy, to offer your bodies as living sacrifices, *holy* and pleasing to God—this is your spiritual act of worship" (emphasis added).

Requirements of the Nazirite

When someone made the choice to take the Vow of the Nazirite, he or she had to live by three requirements: They were to abstain from wine or other fermented drink; they were not to cut their hair; and they were to avoid contact with dead bodies. These requirements were to be kept for the duration of the period of the vow. At the end of that period, they were to appear before the priest at the tabernacle and present their offering to the Lord.

What might these three requirements represent today? The first requirement was abstinence from fermented drink. However, it went even further. Numbers 6:3-4 tells us:

> He must abstain from wine and other fermented drink and must not drink vinegar made from wine or from other fermented drink. He must not drink grape juice or eat grapes or raisins. As long as he is a Nazirite, he must not eat anything that comes from the grapevine, not even the seeds or skins.

Notice that it wasn't enough simply to abstain from fermented drink; the Nazirite had to abstain from anything that was remotely associated with the grapevine. I believe this speaks of our *testimony*. Clearly the Bible does not condemn the drinking of a fermented beverage as sin. However, there may be those who are spiritual infants or the unsaved who have not studied God's Word sufficient-ly to discern the proper conduct of a Christian. Therefore, while it may not be against God's Word to consume a fermented beverage, it may hurt our testimony to those who are not as mature in their faith. We are admonished:

> Do not destroy the work of God for the sake of food. All food is clean, but it is wrong for a man to eat any-thing that causes someone else to stumble. It is bet-ter not to eat meat or drink wine or to do anything else that will cause your brother to fall. (Romans 14:20-12)

It is not enough merely to abstain from the fermented drink; we also must abstain from anything remotely related to the "grapevine." As followers of the Nazarene, we should avoid locations and situations involving the consumption of fermented drinks—even if we aren't directly participating—lest we cause a weaker believer to stumble.

The next Nazirite requirement was to refrain from cutting his or her hair during the duration of the vow. "During the entire period of his vow of separation no razor may be used on his head. He must be holy until the period of his separation to the Lord is over; he must let the hair of his head grow long" (Numbers 6:5). What could this foreshadow for us today? Should we get a new hairstyle and refrain from haircuts? I don't believe that is the application at all. I believe this requirement foreshadows our *witness*.

During the Old Testament period, one could easily point out who had taken the Vow of the Nazirite because of his or her appearance. Long hair was a visible sign of the Nazirite's consecration to the Lord. God wanted the Nazirite to be distinct and noticeable to others. The application: we should not be secret Christians. I am not suggesting that we should wear our hair long or wear a shirt that has "Christian" written across it. What I am advocating is that the world should easi-ly be able to tell that we are followers of Christ. Jesus said, "Let your light shine before men, that they may see your good deeds and praise your Father in heaven" (Matthew 5:16). What Jesus was saying is that the world ought to know that we are His followers by our actions—

our lifestyle. It is lifestyle evangelism. We should conduct ourselves in such a manner that the world will see Christ in us. Those who are lost are not going to read the Bible; therefore, we have to be the *living Bible* for them to read. Just as long hair was a witness to others that the Nazirite had taken a vow to be holy unto God, we should live in a manner that will witness to others and they will know we have vowed to be followers of Christ.

The last requirement deals with avoiding dead bodies: "Throughout the period of his separation to the Lord he must not go near a dead body. Even if his own father or mother or brother or sister dies, he must not make himself ceremonially unclean on account of them" (Numbers 6:6-7a). What could this requirement foreshadow for us today? In Old Testament times, a person was considered ceremonially unclean if he had been exposed to a dead body. Being unclean would prevent him from participating in certain acts of worship. We are told, for example: "The Israelites did everything just as the Lord commanded Moses. But some of them could not celebrate the Passover on that day because they were ceremonially unclean on account of a dead body" (Number 9:5b-6).

Likewise, the priests could not perform their duties if they had become unclean because of a dead body.

> The high priest, the one among his brothers who has had the anointing oil poured on his head and who has been ordained to wear the priestly garments... he must not enter a place where there is a dead body. He must not make himself unclean, even for his father or mother. (Leviticus 21: 10a, 11)

So how does this apply to us today? What makes us unclean before God? Sin does! I believe that as a follower of Christ, we should strive to *live a holy* life—to *avoid sin.* The requirement of the Nazirite to avoid a dead body is an excellent analogy for us concerning the need to avoid sin! Listen to Paul's description of those who are lost: "You were *dead* in your transgressions and sins, in which you used to live when you followed the ways of this world" (Ephesians 2:1-2, emphasis added).

What does our sinful uncleanness do to us? We must take a couple of steps backward to answer that question. We saw how the high priest wasn't able to fulfill his duties if he became unclean. It turns out that if we are followers of Jesus, we too are priests: "But you are a chosen people, a *royal priesthood*, a holy nation, a people belonging to God, that you may declare the praises of him who called you out of darkness into his wonderful light" (1 Peter 2:9, emphasis added).

Our priestly duty is to share the message of Christ with a lost world. Jesus said to the woman at the well, "Everyone who drinks this water will be thirsty again, but whoever drinks the water I give him will never thirst. Indeed, the water I give him will become in him a spring of water welling up to eternal life" (John 4:13-14). Jesus wants to share the "living water" with a lost and dying world, and He uses us as His water containers. The problem with sin is that it makes us unclean (dirty) containers and the world will not drink from dirty containers. Therefore, sin prevents us from fulfilling our priestly roles as suppliers of living water.

If we have professed Christ as our Savior, then we have vowed to be followers of the Nazarene. I believe that the Vow of the Nazirite foreshadows for us how we are to conduct ourselves. The requirement to avoid anything from the grapevine speaks of our testimony. The requirement not to cut one's hair speaks of our witness. And the requirement to avoid dead bodies speaks of our holiness. During the period of the vow, the Nazirite was to be separate, which speaks of our sanctification. And repeating Paul's words: "It is God's will that you should be sanctified...for God did not call us to be impure, but to live a holy life" (1 Thessalonians 4:3,7).

Nazirites in the Scriptures

It turns out that there were three biblical characters who were Nazirites for life. Their parents dedicated them to the Lord before they were born, and the duration of their vow was to be for their entire life!

One was the prophet Samuel. I believe Samuel was a type of a second Nazirite for life—John the Baptist. Samuel was never referred to as a Nazirite; but it can be inferred from the vow his mother took on his behalf before he was born: "O Lord Almighty, if you will only look upon your servant's misery and remember me, and not forget your servant but give her a son, then I will give him to the Lord for all the days of his life, and no razor will ever be used on his head" (1 Samuel 11).

Likewise, John the Baptist was not referred to as a Nazirite; but it can be inferred from the angel's remarks to his father: "Your wife Elizabeth will bear you a son, and you are to give him the name John…He is never to take wine or other fermented drink" (Luke 1:13, 15).

The similarities between these two Nazirites for life are beyond coincidence. Both of their mothers were barren and then blessed with a son through the divine intervention of God. Both men were dedicated for the purpose of being separated and consecrated to God for the duration of their lives. Both were prophets and both had the mission of pointing out the Lord's anointed One. Samuel pointed out David as God's chosen king of Israel and anointed him with oil. John the Baptist pointed out Christ as God's chosen King of Kings. Jesus was baptized and was anointed with the Holy Spirit!

The Tragedy of Broken Vows

The third Nazirite for life is more difficult to understand. He was a judge over Israel whose name was Samson. We need make no inferences as to his being a Nazirite because the Scriptures are very clear on this:

> Then the woman went to her husband and told him, "A man of God came to me. He looked like an angel of God, very awesome. I didn't ask him where he came from, and he didn't tell me his name. But he said to me, 'You will conceive and give birth to a son. Now then, drink no wine or other fermented drink and do not eat anything unclean, because the boy

will be a Nazirite of God from birth until the day of his death.'" (Judges 13:6-7)

Why is Samson so difficult to understand? Because he broke every requirement of the Nazirite vows! He did not keep himself separate, but went to the Philistines to take for himself a Gentile bride. The Scriptures also tell us that on one occasion he killed a lion with his bare hands. Then we are told, "Some time later, when he went back...he turned aside to look at the lion's carcass. In it was a swarm of bees and some honey, which he scooped out with his hands and ate as he went along" (Judges 14:8-9a). This was a breech of the Nazirite vow to avoid a dead body. We are also told that "Samson made a feast there, as was customary for bridegrooms" (Judges 14:10). The customary drink at wedding feasts was wine; although we are not told specifically that Samson drank any wine.

And of course, most of us know the story of how he allowed his hair to be cut as he divulged the secret of his strength to his wicked lover, Delilah. "No razor has ever been used on my head," he said, "because I have been a Nazirite set apart to God since birth. If my head were shaved, my strength would leave me, and I would become as weak as any other man" (Judges 16:17).

After his hair was cut, Samson no longer possessed superhuman strength. But his strength wasn't from his long hair; it was from God. "He awoke from his sleep and thought, 'I'll go out as before and shake myself free.' But he did not know that *the Lord had left him*" (Judges 16:20, emphasis added). His strength had been from the Lord; when the Lord left him, so did his strength!

Now I am going out on a limb here, so follow me closely. I believe the lessons that we learn from Samson are twofold. I believe Samson was both a foreshadowing of Christ and also a foreshadowing for us as followers of Christ. How could Samson be a type of Christ when he behaved so abhorrently? Well Samson is no more a perfect type of Christ than Jonah was. However, just as certain aspects of Jonah's life were prophetic of Christ, the same can be said about certain aspects of Samson's life.

First, consider God's intervention in his birth. Like Christ, it was foretold by an angel. Second, Samson desired to marry a Gentile bride just as Christ came to receive the Church as His Gentile bride. And lastly, it was through his death that Samson had his greatest victory over the enemies of God's people. The Scriptures tell us:

> Now the rulers of the Philistines assembled to offer a great sacrifice to Dagon their god and to celebrate, saying, "Our god has delivered Samson, our enemy, into our hands." Then Samson reached toward the two central pillars on which the temple stood. Bracing himself against them, his right hand on the one and his left hand on the other, Samson said, "Let me die with the Philistines!" Then he pushed with all his might, and down came the temple on the rulers and all the people in it. Thus he killed many more when he died than while he lived. (Judges 16:23, 29-30)

Here we see a foreshadowing that in His death Christ obtained the victory over the enemy—Satan. The writer of Hebrews explains: "Since the children have flesh and blood, he too shared in their humanity so that by his death he might destroy him who holds the power of death—that is, the devil—and free those who all their lives were held in slavery by their fear of death" (Hebrews 2:14-15).

How is Samson also a foreshadowing of how we are to follow Christ? After all, Samson failed all the requirements of the Nazirite. As Christians, followers of the Nazarene, we too are going to fail God. We will find ourselves saying along with Paul: "I do not understand what I do. For what I want to do I do not do, but what I hate I do...For what I do is not the good I want to do; no, the evil I do not want to do—this I keep on doing...What a wretched man I am!" (Romans 7:15,19,24).

The message for us is found in Samson's repentance. "Then Samson prayed to the Lord, 'O Sovereign Lord, remember me'" (Judges 16:28). And because of his repentance, God strengthened him once more and allowed him to have the final victory. What an incredible story of man's failure—juxtaposed by God's grace, mercy, forgiveness, and love! Notice that once again it was *God's strength*—not Samson's—that provided the victory! The application for us is that when we fail God, if we repent and again rely on God's strength He will give us victory over the sin in our lives. We are told: "If we confess our sins, he is faithful and just and will forgive us our sins and purify us from all unrighteousness" (1 John 1:9). Through Christ we have the final victory!

Vows were important in biblical times—and they are still important to us today. New doctors start their profession by making a vow to follow the Oath of Hippocrates. Newly married couples vow to love, honor, and cherish each other. Therefore, new Christians would do well to begin their spiritual life by understanding and following the meaning of the Vow of the Nazirite—a commitment to be a follower of the Nazarene! It involves separation for the purpose of being holy to God. It involves testimony, witness, and holiness. And if we rely upon God's strength—He will give us the final victory!

— CHAPTER TEN QUESTIONS —

1. Read Numbers 6:1-21 concerning the Vow of the Nazirite.

   a. Why do you suppose the vow was given at that time?

   b. Was everyone required to take the vow?

   c. What is the meaning of "separation" in verse 2?

2. Why do you believe the vow was called "Nazirite"? Could there be a connection to Matthew 2:23b? What do you believe Matthew was referring to in 2:23b?

3. The author stated: "I believe that the Vow of the Nazirite passage was a prophecy concerning Jesus the Nazarene and foreshadows what is expected of us if we vow to follow Him." How could the Vow of the Nazirite foreshadow the following aspects of the Christian life?

   a. Sanctification

   b. Witness

   c. Testimony

   d. Holiness

4. Explain why each of the following individuals were or were not Nazirites:

   a. Jesus

   b. John the Baptist

   c. Samson

   d. Samuel

5. Read Numbers 6:13-20 concerning "when the period of his separation is over." If the vow truly is a foreshadowing of the Christian life, explain the possible foreshadowing of the following:

   a. "He is to be brought to the entrance to the Tent of Meeting" (God's dwelling place). Consider 2 Corinthians 5:10.

   b. "The priest is to present them before the Lord." (Consider Hebrews 9:11-15)

   c. "He is to take the hair and put it in the fire." (Consider 1 Corinthians 3:13-15)

6. Read Amos 2:10-13 concerning God's words of judgment upon the nation of Israel.

   a. What sins of the nation did God address?

   b. In verse 12 what do the words "made" and "commanded" imply?

   c. Explain ways that our nation today "makes" and "commands" rules that are contrary to God's Word?

   d. Realizing that the nation of Israel was judged for its wrong doing, what application can be made for our nation today?

ARMAGEDDON

Then they gathered the kings together to the place that in Hebrew is called Armageddon. — Revelation 16:16

On Whit Monday 1725, in Rheims, Nicole Millet was found burnt to death in an unburned chair. Nicole was the wife of the landlord of the Lion d'Or, and her husband, quite naturally, was accused of murdering her and arrested. He was acquitted at his trial when a young surgeon named Nicholas Le Cat convinced the court that not only did Spontaneous Human Combustion occur, but that the Nicole Millet case was a fine example. The final verdict in the case was that Nicole Millet had died "by visitation of God."[1]

Spontaneous Human Combustion is a condition whereby a person spontaneously bursts into flames and is consumed. Although there have been many apparent documented cases of the condition, most people don't believe that it really exists.

In the field of anesthesiology, there is a very rare condition that has been thoroughly studied and proven to exist. It is considered to be the most dreaded potential complication that an anesthesiologist may face—Malignant Hyperthermia. Unlike Spontaneous Human Combustion, patients who develop Malignant Hyperthermia do not erupt into flames and are not consumed. They do, however, generate extremely elevated body temperatures and if left untreated the mortality rate approaches 80 percent. Fortunately, the incidence of

Malignant Hyperthermia is only about 1 in 200,000 anesthetics; and the mortality rate has decreased to less than 10 percent because of an effective treatment.

As effective as the treatment is, however, it continues to have a mortality rate of almost one in ten, which is staggering! Yet, there is a way to decrease the mortality rate to almost zero. It turns out that malignant hyperthermia occurs only when a patient is exposed to certain triggering agents. The triggering agents are well known so by avoiding them, the incidence—and therefore the mortality rate due to malignant hyperthermia—becomes almost nonexistent.

Eternal Hyperthermia

Right now you probably are thinking, "This is interesting but where in the world are you going with this?" I would suggest to you that malignant hyperthermia has a spiritual corollary—"Eternal Hyperthermia." Eternal Hyperthermia is a good description of the eternal ailment awaiting many who will stand before God at the Great White Throne of Judgment. Concerning that day, John the revelator proclaims, "If anyone's name was not found written in the book of life, he was thrown into the lake of fire" (Revelation 20:15).

We don't like to think about the judgment or wrath of God. We would rather concentrate on God's pleasant attributes, like love. After all, "God is love" (1 John 4:16) and "God so loved the world..." (John 3:16). Yet the reality is that Jesus taught more about hell (the place of Eternal Hyperthermia) than He did about heaven! The latter part of John 3:16 goes on to explain why God "gave his one and only Son" —it was so that "whoever believes in him, *shall not perish*" (emphasis added). The fact is, Jesus fervently taught about the place of eternal torment so that those hearing His message would make the decision needed in order to avoid that place!

On one occasion Jesus taught:

> If your hand causes you to sin, cut it off. It is better for you to enter life maimed than with two hands to go into hell, where the fire never goes out. And if your foot causes you to sin, cut it off. It is better for

you to enter life crippled than to have two feet and be thrown into hell. And if your eye causes you to sin, pluck it out. It is better for you to enter the kingdom of God with one eye than to have two eyes and be thrown into hell, where "their worm does not die, and the fire is not quenched." (Mark 9:43-48)

The Judgments

Before condemning anyone to suffer Eternal Hyperthermia, God will sit in judgment over all people. The Scriptures actually describe two different judgments. The "Great White Throne Judgment" occurs after the millennial reign of Christ. Concerning those who have not received Christ as their Savior, we are told, "The dead were judged according to what they had done as recorded in the books" (Revelation 20:12). There is also the "Judgment Seat of Christ." This is a judgment of those who have received Christ as their Savior. Paul asserts: "For we must all appear before the judgment seat of Christ, that each one may receive what is due him for the things done while in the body, whether good or bad" (2 Corinthians 5:10). The Judgment Seat of Christ will occur after the Church has been "raptured," at the beginning of the seven-year period known as the "Tribulation."

While those who have been raptured are being judged and given their just rewards in heaven, on earth there will be a time of Tribulation, when God will pour out His wrath on those who have rejected Him. This seven-year period will culminate in a great battle called Armageddon. *The Battle of Armageddon will be the final triumph of Christ over the enemies of God during this age.*

The Judgments and Prophecy

There are many prophetic Old Testament passages that are fulfilled in the Tribulation, as described in the Book of Revelation. Ezekiel called the Second Coming of Christ the "Day of the Lord," and said it would be "a time of doom for all nations" (Ezekiel 30:3). The Tribulation was what Daniel described as the seventieth week, when "War will continue until the end, and desolations have been decreed" (Daniel 9:26).

There is another Old Testament passage that foreshadows the Tribulation and Battle of Armageddon in great detail, perhaps more so than any other prophetic passage. Yet it lies buried in a little-studied book of the Bible and its significance usually goes unnoticed. I accidentally stumbled across an understanding of this little-known passage some time ago. Now it is my privilege to be your guide on this journey into the foreshadowing of Armageddon.

To uncover this passage and excavate its meaning, we need to approach it in the manner of an archaeologist. When an archaeologist begins to search for a buried artifact, he doesn't just arbitrarily dig anywhere; he follows clues to increase his likelihood of making a find. The Old Testament is a vast area in which to search for a foreshadowing of Armageddon. If we are to have success, we too need a clue that will lead us to a specific passage in which to dig deeper for our prophetic foreshadowing.

The prophet Isaiah gives us the clue that we seek. Isaiah proclaimed in a well-known passage: "For to us a child is born, to us a son is given, and the government will be on his shoulders. And he will be called Wonderful Counselor, Mighty God, Everlasting Father, Prince of Peace" (Isaiah 9:6). We often quote this verse at Christmas each year, when we commemorate the birth of the Christ-child. But a correct handling of this prophecy also speaks of the Second Coming of Christ. True, it mentions that He will be born as a child—a reference to His incarnation; however, we can't overlook the rest of the passage. It tells us: "Of the increase of his government and peace there will be no end. He will reign on David's throne and over his kingdom, establishing and upholding it with justice and righteousness from that time on and forever" (Isaiah 9:7).

Certainly Isaiah seems to be including the entire manifestation of the incarnation—both Christ's birth and His kingly rule (a Second Coming role). Why is this important to our study? Because of the context in which Isaiah makes this prophecy. Seldom does anyone include the entire context that Isaiah intended. To see the big picture that Isaiah was trying to show us, we need to back up two verses.

> For as in the day of Midian's defeat, you have shattered the yoke that burdens them, the bar across their shoulders, the rod of their oppressor. Every warrior's boot used in battle and every garment rolled in blood will be destined for burning, will be fuel for the fire. For unto us a child is born.... (Isaiah 9:4-6)

Now we have the clue we need to guide us to the proper place to dig for more information. The context that Isaiah intended when giving this prophecy about Christ involves a battle where the enemies of the victor are defeated and destined to burn in a fire! And who is the victor that Isaiah described? The victor is Jesus Christ who would be born as the Christ-child! We know, by putting this together with information from the Book of Revelation, that the great battle where Christ defeats the enemies of God—and afterwards His enemies are thrown into the lake of fire—is called the battle of Armageddon!

So, here is a clue to help us find more information that might serve to foreshadow the events of the tribulation and the Battle of Armageddon. Our clue is when Isaiah says, "as in the day of Midian's defeat." Now all we have to do is find a passage concerning Midian's defeat, and we might be able to unearth some prophecy concerning the Second Coming of Christ, including the Tribulation and the Battle of Armageddon!

The Book of Judges

It turns out that a description of Midian's defeat is found in the Old Testament Book of Judges. Let's travel back and see if we can find a foreshadowing of the Tribulation and the Battle of Armageddon. Before we break ground and start digging, let's take a step back and survey the lay of the land.

The Book of Judges portrays the period between Israel's conquest of the land of Canaan and the reign of their first king. It was a time when great leaders, who were known as "judges," led the Israelites.

These judges were not like our current concept of a judge—individuals who decide issues of law. Instead, they were military leaders—"deliverers." A repeating cycle of events reoccurs throughout the Book of Judges; in that repetitious cycle, we get our first glimpse of the prophetic foreshadowing that God wants us to understand.

The cycle begins after the death of Joshua when we are told:

> After that whole generation had been gathered to their fathers, another generation grew up, who knew neither the Lord nor what he had done for Israel. Then the Israelites did evil in the eyes of the Lord and served the Baals. They forsook the Lord, the God of their fathers, who had brought them out of Egypt. They followed and worshiped various gods of the peoples around them. They provoked the Lord to anger because they forsook him and served Baal and the Ashtoreths. In his anger against Israel the Lord handed them over to raiders who plundered them. He sold them to their enemies all around, whom they were no longer able to resist. Whenever Israel went out to fight, the hand of the Lord was against them to defeat them, just as he had sworn to them. They were in great distress.
>
> Then the Lord raised up judges, who saved them out of the hands of these raiders... Whenever the Lord raised up a judge for them, he was with the judge and saved them out of the hands of their enemies as long as the judge lived; for the Lord had compassion on them as they groaned under those who oppressed and afflicted them. But when the judge died, the people returned to ways even more corrupt than those of their fathers, following other gods and serving and worshipping them. (Judges 2:11-16,18-19)

This repeating cycle of events is prophetically significant (See Table 1 on page 210). By repeating this cycle over and over again throughout Judges, we can infer that God especially wants us to take notice of these events. First, the cycle starts with God's people dwelling in the Promised Land. Throughout the Scriptures, the Promised Land is often used symbolically to represent heaven or our spiritual life. By having the setting of the Promised Land at the beginning of this repeating cycle, we are reminded that man began his history in the Garden of Eden, where he enjoyed a perfect fellowship with God.

The next event in this repeating cycle is that God's people fall away from following Him and begin to worship the idols of the surrounding nations. Here we see a reference to the fall of man when Adam and Eve believed the lies of Satan instead of obeying the commands of God.

Next in the cycle, God allows an enemy to oppress the Israelites. This would represent the fallen condition of man and his oppression by the enemy—Satan. During their oppression, the Israelites would cry out to God; He would then raise up a deliverer to defeat the enemy of His people. It is here that we see the need for repentance if man is to be saved from sin's oppression. The deliverer that these judges foreshadowed is Jesus Christ who ultimately will defeat the enemy at His Second Coming.

After the enemy was defeated, God's people enjoyed peace for "as long as the judge lived." Here we see a foreshadowing of the millennial reign of Christ and heaven. It will be a day of perfect peace when "He will wipe every tear from their eyes. There will be no more death or mourning or crying or pain, for the old order of things has passed away" (Revelation 21:4). And please do not overlook the duration of this time of perfect peace—*as long as the judge lived.* Jesus will live forever; those who have received Him as their personal deliverer will live with Him in perfect peace for all eternity.

We have surveyed the lay of the land, and understand that the Book of Judges is representative of a repetitive cycle of events that gives an overview of the fall of man, the need for repentance, the victory of Christ, and the perfect peace of heaven. Now we are ready to dig into the description of Midian's defeat and see what God has foreshadowed concerning the Tribulation and the Battle of Armageddon. Midian's defeat is portrayed for us in Judges chapters 6, 7, and 8.

Gideon — Mighty Warrior

The judge who defeated the Midianites was Gideon. When we are first introduced to him, he is doing something strange. We are told:

> The angel of the Lord came and sat down under the oak in Ophrah that belonged to Joash the Abiezrite, where his son Gideon was threshing wheat in a winepress to keep it from the Midianites. When the angel of the Lord appeared to Gideon, he said, "The Lord is with you, mighty warrior." (Judges 6:11-12)

The great importance of this passage is evident by the presence of an awesome Old Testament figure—"the Angel of the Lord." As we discussed in earlier chapters, many believe that the Angel of the Lord was none other than a pre-incarnate manifestation of Christ Himself. If this is the case, and I personally believe that it is, then Christ is personally orchestrating these events. He is revealing to us information about Himself and what He would do in the future. If the Angel of the Lord is indeed Christ, then when he says to Gideon, "The Lord is with you," His statement was a *literal reality*—the Lord was literally with him!

Here we might think that God has a sense of humor. Gideon was threshing wheat, hiding in a winepress when the Angel of the Lord heralds him as "Mighty Warrior!" Threshing wheat in a winepress was odd; obviously, wheat was not threshed in a winepress under normal conditions! A winepress was an enclosed structure where grapes were trampled so their juice could be collected. Wheat, on the other hand, was threshed out in the open, where it could be tossed into the air and the chaff blown away. We are told that Gideon was threshing the wheat in the winepress because he was hiding from the Midianites.

If we make a careful search of the Scriptures and look for something foreshadowed that combines a reference to wheat and a winepress, we find it in the Book of Revelation. Concerning the Second Coming of Christ, the Scriptures tell us:

> I looked, and there before me was a white cloud, and seated on the cloud was one "like a son of man" with

a crown of gold on his head and a sharp sickle in his hand. Then another angel came out of the temple and called in a loud voice to him who was sitting on the cloud, "Take your sickle and reap, because the time to reap has come, for the harvest of the earth is ripe." So he who was seated on the cloud swung his sickle over the earth, and the earth was harvested. Another angel came out of the temple in heaven, and he too had a sharp sickle. Still another angel, who had charge of the fire, came from the altar and called in a loud voice to him who had the sharp sickle, "Take your sharp sickle and gather the clusters of grapes from the earth's vine, because its grapes are ripe." The angel swung his sickle on the earth, gathered its grapes and threw them into the great winepress of God's wrath. They were trampled in the winepress outside the city, and blood flowed out of the press, rising as high as the horse's bridal for a distance of 1,600 stadia. (Revelation 14:14-20)

Here we find that mankind is harvested with a sickle (like wheat), and then trampled in the great winepress of God's wrath. Revelation prophesies that Christ will accomplish this during the time of His Second Coming, when He returns riding on the cloud. This was partially foreshadowed for us by Gideon. As the judge in this particular cycle, Gideon symbolically represents the "deliverer"—Jesus Christ.

A Prophet Prepares the Way

Let's see if we can uncover additional evidence in this passage to foreshadow Christ. Notice that just as God sent a prophet, John the Baptist, to prepare the way for Christ—we are told likewise that the Lord sent a prophet to His people just before Gideon became their judge.

When the Israelites cried to the Lord because of Midian, he sent them a prophet, who said, "This is what the Lord, the God of Israel, says: I brought you up out of Egypt, out of the land of slavery. I snatched you from the power of Egypt and from the hand of all your oppressors. I drove them from before you and gave you their land. I said to you, "I am the Lord your God; do not worship the gods of the Amorites, in whose land you live." But you have not listened to me. (Judges 6:7-10)

The Sign of the Passover Offering

After meeting the Angel of the Lord, Gideon asked for a sign to verify the angel's identity. "Gideon replied, 'If now I have found favor in your eyes, give me a sign that it is really you talking to me'" (Judges 6:17). Gideon then asked the Angel of the Lord to wait while he prepared for him an offering:

Gideon went in, prepared a young goat, and from an ephah of flour he made bread without yeast…The angel of God said to him, "Take the meat and the unleavened bread, place them on this rock, and pour out the broth." And Gideon did so. With the tip of the staff that was in his hand, the angel of the Lord touched the meat and the unleavened bread. Fire flared from the rock, consuming the meat and the bread. And the angel of the Lord disappeared. (Verses 19-21)

This offering, consisting of a young goat or lamb and unleavened bread, was the Passover offering. Therefore the sign, which proved the Angel of the Lord's identity, *was the consumption of the Passover offering!* Here we see the proof of Christ's identity. Christ proved Himself when He came and fulfilled His role as the Passover Lamb—*the Lamb of God who takes away the sins of the world.* This revelation caused Gideon to build an altar to the Lord. "So Gideon built an altar to the Lord there and called it The Lord is Peace" (Judges 6:24).

The Sign of the Fleece

After receiving the sign proving the identity of the Angel of the Lord, Gideon then asks for a twofold sign of assurance of his victory over the Midianites:

Gideon said to God, "If you will save Israel by my hand as you have promised—look, I will place a wool fleece on the threshing floor. If there is dew only on the fleece and all the ground is dry, then I will know that you will save Israel by my hand, as you said." And that is what happened. Gideon rose early the next day; he squeezed the fleece and wrung out the dew—a bowlful of water. Then Gideon said to God, "Do not be angry with me. Let me make just one more request. Allow me one more test with the fleece. This time make the fleece dry and the ground covered with dew." That night God did so. Only the fleece was dry; all the ground was covered with dew. (Judges 6:36-40)

What could this twofold sign of the fleece represent? It reminds us of the two comings of Christ. The sign guaranteeing an assurance of victory over the enemy represents for us the Second Coming of Christ. The wool fleece then would symbolically represent Christ as the Lamb of God.

The *first time* the fleece was wet and the ground was dry. Here we see that when Christ first came to earth and fulfilled His role as the sacrificial lamb, it was His blood that was shed. But the second time, the fleece was dry while the ground was wet. Here we see foreshadowed Christ's return at His Second Coming. At that time, His blood will not be shed, but the ground will be wet with the blood of men. "They were trampled in the winepress outside the city, and blood flowed out of the press, rising as high as the horse's bridles for a distance of 1,600 stadia" (Revelation 14:20).

Tribulation and Armageddon Foreshadowed

So far, our dig has yielded much foreshadowing regarding Christ in this account of Gideon's defeat of the Midianites (See Table 2 on page 211). Now let's begin searching for artifacts that may foreshadow the events of the Tribulation, specifically the Battle of Armageddon. Instead of artifacts, we can call them "tribfacts!" Before we can match tribfacts from the Book of Judges with

Tribulation events mentioned in the Book of Revelation, we must know what to look for. (See Table 3 on page 212 for a list of the events of the tribulation.)

Now that we are armed with the details, let's start digging. In the very first verse of Judges 6, we find our first tribfact: "Again the Israelites did evil in the eyes of the Lord, and *for seven years* he gave them into the hands of the Midianites" (Judges 6:1, emphasis added). How perfect it is that "as in the day of Midian's defeat," the Israelites suffered for a seven-year period of oppression, foreshadowing perfectly for us the seven-year period of the Tribulation.

We need only read the next verse to find our next tribfact. "Because the power of Midian was so oppressive, the Israelites prepared shelters for themselves in mountain clefts, caves and strongholds" (Judges 6:2). Here we see a foreshadowing of the sixth seal: "I watched as he opened the sixth seal... Then the kings of the earth, the princes, the generals, the rich, the mighty, and every slave and every free man *hid in caves and among the rocks of the mountains*" (Revelation 6:12,15, emphasis added).

In verse three, we are told: "Whenever the Israelites planted their crops, the Midianites, Amalekites and *other eastern peoples* invaded the country" (emphasis added). Here we have a foreshadowing of the sixth bowl: "The sixth angel poured out his bowl on the great river Euphrates, and its water was dried up to prepare the way for the *kings from the East*" (Revelation 16:12, emphasis added).

We need look only as far as the next two verses of Judges 6, to see our next Tribfact:

> They camped on the land and ruined the crops all the way to Gaza and did not spare a living thing for Israel, neither sheep nor cattle nor donkeys. They came up with their livestock and their tents *like swarms of locusts*. It was impossible to count the men and their camels; they invaded the land to ravage it. (Judges 6:4-5, emphasis added)

Their description as "swarms of locusts" foreshadows for us what Revelation calls the fifth trumpet:

The fifth angel sounded his trumpet, and I saw a star that had fallen from the sky to the earth. The star was given the key to the shaft of the Abyss. When he opened the Abyss, smoke rose from it like the smoke from a gigantic furnace...And out of the smoke locusts came down upon the earth and were given power like that of scorpions of the earth...The locusts looked like horses prepared for battle. On their heads they wore something like crowns of gold, and their faces resembled human faces. (Revelation 9:1-2,3,7)

The prophet Joel also prophesied concerning the invasion of the locusts:

What the locust swarm has left the great locusts have eaten; what the great locusts have left the young locusts have eaten; what the young locusts have left other locusts have eaten... A nation has invaded my land, powerful and without number; it has the teeth of a lion, the fangs of a lioness. (Joel 1:4,6)

Our next tribfact involves the location of Gideon's battle against the enemies of God's people. Judges 6:33 tells us: "Now all the Midianites, Amalekites and other eastern peoples joined forces and crossed over the Jordan and camped in the Valley of Jezreel." Here we are given a foreshadowing of the final great battle that will bring the Tribulation period to a close—Armageddon. "Then they gathered the kings together to the place that in Hebrew is called Armageddon" (Revelation 16:16).

The word "Armageddon" is Hebrew for Mount Megiddo. This mountain overlooks at its base a flat plain called the Valley of Jezreel. In other words, as the Midianites and their allies were gathering in the Valley of Jezreel at the foot of Mount Megiddo, they were gathering in the very same place where the Book of Revelation foretells that the Battle of Armageddon will occur! How accurately God foretells for us the events of the Tribulation, even the very location that the final battle will occur! Only God could orchestrate events of history so intricately!

Next, let us focus on the events of the battle. God had Gideon do something very strange. He told Gideon to gather all of the men together. Of the men who reported to fight on behalf of Israel, Gideon told those who trembled with fear to leave. Twenty-two thousand soldiers left—leaving only ten thousand. Of the ten thousand remaining, the Scripture tells us:

> Gideon took the men down to the water. There the Lord told him, "Separate those who lap the water with their tongues like a dog from those who kneel down to drink." Three hundred men lapped with their hands to their mouths. All the rest got down on their knees to drink. The Lord said to Gideon, "With the three hundred men that lapped I will save you and give the Midianites into your hands. (Judges 7:5-7)

Three hundred men would do battle against an army with the following description: "The Midianites, the Amalekites and all the other eastern peoples had settled in the valley, thick as locusts. Their camels could no more be counted than the sand on the seashore" (Judges 7:12). Why would God send only three hundred men against such a vast army? I'll let God answer that question: "In order that Israel may not boast against me that her own strength has saved her" (Judges 7:2b). This battle was the Lord's! It wasn't the strength of Israel that would cause victory on this day—it was the strength of the Lord.

This foreshadows for us the Battle of Armageddon. John the revelator gives us the details of the battle:

> I saw heaven standing open and there before me was a white horse, whose rider is called Faithful and True...He is dressed in a robe dipped in blood, and his name is the Word of God. The armies of heaven were following him, riding on white horses and dressed in fine linen, white and clean. Out of his mouth comes a sharp sword with which to strike down the nations. (Revelation 19:11,13-15)

The armies of heaven are following Christ; but they won't have to worry about damaging their fine white linen garments because Christ defeats the enemies with the sword from His mouth! Just as it was the Lord who defeated the enemy in the day of Gideon—so shall it be at the Battle of Armageddon.

So, we see that Gideon took the three hundred men and divided them into three groups. This may symbolically represent the three groups of judgments during the time of the Tribulation: the seals, trumpets, and bowls. Because the seals are mentioned before the trumpets, which are then followed by details of the bowls, many people believe that the events of these three judgments will occur chronologically.

However, because some of the bowl judgments seem to be completions of the trumpet judgments, some believe that the three groups of judgments occur concurrently. For example, the second trumpet causes the destruction of one-third of the sea life and the second bowl causes the destruction of the remaining sea life.

However, if you consider that seven seals secured the scroll, after the seventh seal was broken, the complete contents of the scroll could be known. It may be that the trumpet and bowl judgments are the contents of the seven-sealed scroll. So after the seventh seal was broken, the contents containing the trumpet and bowl judgments could then be activated and occur concurrently. Giving credibility to this hypothesis is the fact that the seventh of each of the judgments is the same event: thunder, lightning, and an earthquake.

Since the final event of each judgment is the same, it may be that they are actually the same final event. How could this one final event be foreshadowed in Gideon's defeat of the Midianites? Looking closely at the details of the battle we can find the answer.

Gideon had his three groups of one hundred men surround the Midianite camp in the dark of night. They each carried a trumpet and a torch hidden inside of a clay jar. On Gideon's command, they all blew their trumpets, pulled out the torches, and then smashed their jars. As the Midianites were caught unaware in the middle of the night, the sudden blowing of three hundred trumpets must have sounded to them like a great thunder. As the torches were pulled out from inside the clay jars, the sudden brightness might have appeared to them as lightning. And finally, as the three hundred clay jars were smashed to the ground, it may have felt like an earthquake!

All the way back in the time of the Judges, God foreshadowed for us the final events of the Tribulation—on the exact spot where the Battle of Armageddon will transpire! After the trumpets sounded, the torches were exposed, and the jars were broken, the Midianites began killing one another. "When the three hundred trumpets sounded, the Lord caused the men throughout the camp to turn on each other with their swords" (Judges 7:22). This was a foreshadowing of the second seal: "Then another horse came out, a fiery red one. Its rider was given power to take peace from the earth and to *make men slay each other*" (Revelation 6:4, emphasis added).

At the end of the Tribulation period, Satan is not destroyed—he is only incarcerated:

> He seized the dragon, that ancient serpent, who is the devil, or Satan, and bound him for a thousand years. He threw him into the Abyss, and locked and sealed it over him, to keep him from deceiving the nations anymore until the thousand years were ended. (Revelation 20:2-3)

Although Satan is not destroyed at the conclusion of the Tribulation, his two leaders are destroyed:

> But the beast was captured, and with him the false prophet who had performed the miraculous signs on his behalf...The two of them were thrown alive into the fiery lake of burning sulfur. (Revelation 19:20)

The destruction of two enemy leaders was foreshadowed by Gideon's defeat of the Midianites as well: "They also captured two of the Midianite leaders, Oreb and Zeeb. They killed Oreb at the rock of Oreb, and Zeeb at the winepress of Zeeb" (Judges 7:25). (See Table 4 on page 213 for an overview of our dig for tribfacts.)

The end of the line for the two leaders of Satan (the beast and the false prophet) meant spending eternity in the fiery lake of burning sulfur—Eternal Hyperthermia!

It will also be the final destination for all who have not received Christ as Savior. The mortality rate of Eternal Hyperthermia is 100 percent and there will never be a cure. However, as with the medical condition of malignant hyperthermia, the mortality rate can be literally reduced to zero by avoiding the condition altogether! The way to avoid Eternal Hyperthermia is to receive the gift of salvation that Christ freely offers to anyone who will accept it. The inoculation that makes us immune to the spiritual illness of Eternal Hyperthermia is found in the following verse: "If you confess with your mouth, 'Jesus is Lord,' and believe in your heart that God raised him from the dead, you will be saved" (Romans 10:9). If you haven't received this inoculation already, I pray that you will receive it while there is still time!

Table 1

PROPHETIC CYCLE OF JUDGES

REPEATING CYCLE	POSSIBLE PROPHETIC MEANING
1. God's people are in the Promised Land.	1. Man started out in heaven.
2. God's people fall away from God.	2. The fall of man.
3. God allows an enemy to oppress them.	3. Satan is the oppressor.
4. God's people cry out to Him.	4. Repentance is required.
5. God raises up a deliverer to defeat the enemy of His people.	5. Christ is the deliverer.
6. The oppressor is defeated.	6. Christ defeats Satan at His Second Coming.
7. God's people have a time of peace for as long as the judge lived.	7. Christ's millennial reign and heaven.

Table 2

FORESHADOWING OF CHRIST

PROPHECY	SHADOW
1. "As in the day of Midian's defeat" and "unto us a child is born" (Isaiah 9:4).	1. Christ Child
2. The Angel of the Lord.	2. Pre-incarnate manifestation of Christ.
3. Gideon—the judge who would deliver the Israelites from the oppression of their enemy.	3. Christ is our deliverer from the oppression of the enemy—Satan.
4. "Threshing wheat in a winepress" (Judges 6:11).	4. "Son of man with a crown of gold on his head and a sharp sickle in his hand" (Rev. 14:14).
5. Proof of the identity of the Angel of the Lord = Passover offering.	5. Proof of Christ's identity = fulfillment of His role as the Passover Lamb.
6. Assurance of victory against the enemy = twofold sign of the fleece.	6. Assurance of Christ's victory against Satan = His Second Coming.

TABLE 3

EVENTS OF THE TRIBULATION – DANIEL'S 70TH WEEK OF YEARS

SEVEN SEALED SCROLL	SEVEN TRUMPETS	SEVEN BOWLS
1ST SEAL – rider on a white horse wearing a crown and holding a bow; bent on conquest.	**1ST TRUMPET** – hail, fire, and blood resulting in the burning of one-third of the grass and trees.	**1ST BOWL** – malignant sores on those with the mark of the beast.
2ND SEAL – rider on a red horse with a large sword; the power to make men slay each other.	**2ND TRUMPET** – volcano thrown into the sea. One-third of sea turned to blood destroying one-third of sea life and one-third of ships.	**2ND BOWL** – rest of sea turned to blood resulting in death of the rest of sea life.
3RD SEAL – rider on a black horse holding a pair of scales. Do not damage the oil and wine.	**3RD TRUMPET** – meteorite "Wormwood" falls into fresh water and one-third of it turns bitter and kills those who drink it.	**3RD BOWL** – the rest of the fresh water rivers and springs are turned to blood.
4TH SEAL – rider on a pale horse whose name is Death, Hades followed close behind. One-fourth of the earth killed.	**4TH TRUMPET** – one-third of sun, stars, and moon darkened.	**4TH BOWL** – mankind is scorched with intense fire and heat from the sun. They still refuse to repent and glorify God.
5TH SEAL – souls of those who were martyred. Told to wait until the full number is complete.	**5TH TRUMPET** – torture of those not having the seal of God by demons that resemble scorpions. Men will seek death but not find it.	**5TH BOWL** – poured out on the throne of the beast causing darkness and pain.
6TH SEAL – sun turned black, moon turned red, and stars fall to earth. Men hide in caves.	**6TH TRUMPET**– slaughter of one-third of human population by 200 million demonic horsemen released by four angels.	**6TH BOWL** – river Euphrates dried up to prepare way for the kings from the east. Battle of Armageddon.
7TH SEAL – "Silence in heaven" followed by thunder, lightning, and an earthquake.	**7TH TRUMPET** – "The kingdom of the world has become the kingdom of our Lord and of his Christ," thunder, lightning, and an earthquake.	**7TH BOWL** – "It is done" thunder, lightning, and an earthquake.

TABLE 4

EVENTS OF THE TRIBULATION
As Foreshadowed by Gideon's Defeat of the Midianites

Events from the Book of Judges

- 7-year period of oppression (Judges 6:1)
- Men fled to caves (Judges 6:2)
- Invaders from the east (Judges 6:3)
- Described as a swarm of locusts (Judges 6:5)
- Site of the battle = Valley of Jezreel (Judges 6:33)
- Three groups of warriors (Judges 7:16)
- Trumpets, torches, and smashing of jars (Judges 7:20)
- Midianites turned their swords on one another (Judges 7:22)
- Death of two leaders: Oreb and Zeeb (Judges 7:25)

Events from the Book of Revelation

- Daniel's seventieth week (Daniel 9)
- 6th seal (Revelation 6:12)
- 6th bowl (Revelation 16:12)
- 5th trumpet (Revelation 9:1)
- Armageddon (Revelation 16:16)
- Three groups of judgments: seals, trumpets, and bowls (Revelation 6–9, 16)
- Thunder, lightning, and an earthquake
- 2nd seal (Revelation 6:3)
- Death of Satan's leaders: beast and false prophet (Revelation 19:20)

— CHAPTER ELEVEN QUESTIONS —

1. Look at Isaiah 9:2-7:

   a. Isaiah said "on those living in the land of the shadow of death a light has dawned." What did Isaiah mean by "the land of the shadow of death"? What did he mean by "a light has dawned"?

   b. Do the events in verses 4-5 describe Christ's First or Second Advent?

2. Read Judges 2:10-19 concerning the repeating cycle of events that transpired.

   a. How was it a foreshadowing of humanity's relationship with God?

   b. Who does the enemy foreshadow?

   c. What was required for God to raise up a judge?

   d. Who did the judge foreshadow?

   e. What stage in the cycle do you believe our nation is in today?

3. Review Judges 6 and explain how Christ was foreshadowed by the following:

   a. Gideon

   b. "threshing wheat in a winepress"

   c. "The Lord is with you"

   d. "[goat] meat and the unleavened bread"

   e. two fold sign of the fleece

4. Review Table 3 and match the following events with the corresponding tribulation event:

a. "for seven years he gave them into the hands of the Midianites"

b. "the Israelites prepared shelters for themselves in mountain clefts, caves and strongholds"

c. "the Midianites. Amalekites and other eastern peoples invaded their country"

d. "like swarms of locusts"

e. "the Lord caused the men throughout the camp to turn on each other with their swords"

5. Explain how the following events in the Battle of Armageddon were foreshadowed in Judges 6—8:
   a. The location of the battle
   b. The origin of the enemies of God
   c. The three groups of judgments
   d. Thunder, lightning and an earthquake
   e. The source of the victory
   f. The death of the two leaders

6. Take a look at Judges 7:1-8 concerning the men who were chosen for battle.
   a. If Gideon foreshadows Christ, whom might the twenty-two thousand men who left foreshadow?
   b. What was the message of this reduction in the number of men? (See 7:2)

—END NOTES —

Introduction

1. Harold Bloom, Shakespeare: *The Invention of the Human* (New York: Riverhead Books, 1998), 215.

Chapter One: Healing From a Shadow

1. Ada R. Habershon, *Study of the Types* (Grand Rapids, Mich.: Kregel Publications, 1997), 9.

2. Habershon, 11

3. Clarence Larkin, *Dispensational Truth* (Rev. Clarence Larkin, Est., 1920), 153.

4. Robert Strand, *365 Days to Cherish* (Green Forest, Ark.: New Leaf Press, 1997) November 10—The Train Stops Just in Time.

Chapter Two: The Lamb of God

1. Charlotte Elliott, "Just As I Am Without One Plea," P.D.

2. Arthur Pink, *Gleanings in Genesis* (Chicago: The Moody Bible Institute, 1922), 221.

3. Pink, 222

4. Pink, 222

5. *Nelson's New Illustrated Bible Dictionary* (Nashville: Thomas Nelson Publishers, 1995), 56.

6. Grant R. Jeffrey, *Armageddon, Appointment with Destiny* (Tulsa, Okla.: Frontier Research Publications, Inc., 1997), 29.

7. Mitch and Zhava Glaser, *The Fall Feasts of Israel* (Chicago: The Moody Bible Institute, 1987), 89.

8. Glaser, 89-90.

Chapter Three: Spiritual Sustenance

1. Harold J. Chadwick, *The New Foxe's Book of Martyrs* (Gainesville, Fla.: Bridge-Logos Publishers, 1997), 99.

2. *Nelson's New Illustrated Bible Dictionary* (Nashville: Thomas Nelson Publishers, 1995), 819, 1114.

3. *Ibid,* 819.

Chapter Four: The Spring Feasts

1. Washington Irving, *George Washington: A Biography* (Cambridge, Mass.: Da Capo Press, 1975) 713-716.

2. John Hagee, *Final Dawn Over Jerusalem* (Nashville: Thomas Nelson Publishers, 1979), 167.

3. Grant R. Jeffrey, *Armageddon: Appointment with Destiny* (Tulsa, Okla.: Frontier Research Publications, 1997), 45.

4. Ada R. Habershon, *Study of the Types* (Grand Rapids, Mich.: Kregel Publications, 1997), 37-38.

5. Kevin Howard and Marvin Rosenthal, *The Feasts of the Lord* (Nashville: Thomas Nelson Publishers, 1997), 54.

6. Howard and Rosenthal, 55.

7. Howard and Rosenthal, 57.

8. Howard and Rosenthal, 59.

9. Alfred Edersheim, *The Temple* (Grand Rapids, Mich.: Kregel Publications, 1997) 144.

10. C. H. Spurgeon, *Christ in the Old Testament* (Chattanooga, Tenn.: AMG Publishers, 1994) 380.

11. Fanny J. Crosby, "Redeemed, How I Love to Proclaim It," P.D.

12. Howard and Rosenthal, 67.

13. Hagee, 173.

14. Jeffrey, 57.

15. Jeffrey, 57.

16. Howard and Rosenthal, 15.

17. Hagee, 176.

18. Jeffrey, 59.

19. Howard and Rosenthal, 86.

20. Hagee, 177.

21. Jeffrey, 65.

22. *Ibid.*, 64.

Chapter Five: The Fall Feasts

1. American Academy of Achievement, The Hall of Science and Exploration, "Jonas Salk, M.D., Developer of Polio Vaccine," Biography, Internet article www.achievement.org/autodoc/page/ sal10bio-

2. Glaser, 16.

3. Howard and Rosenthal, 105.

4. Howard and Rosenthal, 113.

5. Hagee, 183-184.

6. Glaser, The Fall Feasts of Israel, 85.

7. Howard & Rosenthal, The Feasts of the Lord, 119.

8. Glaser, The Fall Feasts of Israel, 149.

9. Glaser, 163.

10. Howard & Rosenthal, The Feasts of the Lord, 135.

11. Jeffrey, 197-198.

12. Howard and Rosenthal, 138.

13. Howard and Rosenthal, 140.

Chapter Six: Immanuel

1. Geneva Tabernacle model, Internet article. Page authored by Martyn Barrow, www.domini.org/tabern/tabhome.htm

Chapter Seven: The Bridegroom

1. The Discoverers of Anesthesia, IV, "Does Your Mother Know Your Out? The Story of Dr. James Y. Simpson", December 1981, *Resident & Staff Physician*, 29-31.

2. *The Random House Dictionary* (New York: Random House Inc., 1980), 327.

3. Edward E. Hindson, *The Philistines and the Old Testament* (Grand Rapids, Mich.: Baker Book House Company, 1971), 155-156.

4. Hindson, 32.

5. Hindson, 156.

Chapter Eight: Joshua

1. Warren W. Wiersbe, *Be Strong, an Old Testament Study Joshua* (Colorado Springs: Chariot Victor Publishing, 1993), 65.

2. Wiersbe, 17.

Chapter Nine: Zaphenath - Paneah

1. Lucy Frank Scquire, M.D., *Fundamentals of Radiology*, Fourth Edition (Cambridge, Mass.: Harvard University Press, 1988), 1.

2. Scquire, 23.

3. Pink, 343.

4. *Ibid.*, 357.

5. *Ibid.*, 360.

Chapter Eleven: Armageddon

1. Garth Haslam, Anomailes, "Spontaneous Human Combustion, Nicole Millet Case" (Internet Article) ww.sonic.net/~anomaly

—ABOUT THE AUTHOR —

*T*homas Cash resides in Birmingham, Alabama with his wife Beth and their two children, Alison and Joseph. He practices Anesthesiology at HealthSouth Medical Center and teaches an adult Bible study at Lakeside Baptist Church.

Dr. Cash enjoys mountain biking, sailing, and snow skiing. His passion is studying God's Word.

Notes

Notes

Notes

Notes

Printed in the United States
75734LV00003B/58-105